Love Guru

Love Guru

More than 1,000 tips on the mysteries of love and success

MK Mazumdar

MP

MAHAVEER PUBLISHERS

Published by
MAHAVEER PUBLISHERS
4675A-21, Second Floor, Ansari Road,
Daryaganj, New Delhi – 110002
Ph. : 011 – 66629669–89, 23244999
e-mail : mahaveerpublishers@gmail.com
website : www.mahaveerpublishers.com

First Edition : 2010
5th Impression : 2015

Love Guru
ISBN (10) : 8183520081
ISBN (13) : 9788183520089

Distributed in India by
VAIBHAV BOOK SERVICE
e-mail : vaibhavbookservice@gmail.com

Distributed in Nepal by
BAJRANGBALI BOOK ENTERPRISES PVT. LTD.
Jyatha Mushyabahal, Ward No. 27, Kathmandu, Nepal
e-mail : bajrangbalibooks@gmail.com

Printed in India

Pothee padh padh jag muaa,
pandit bhaya na koi;
Dhai akhar prem ka,
padhe so pandit hoi.

—Kabir

Contents

1
What is Love

Love, affection and passion are things that make a person imaginative. As soon as someone steps into the threshold of teenage, the world of dreams starts swimming in front of the eyes. In these dreams, there is a desire to acquire somebody, to like somebody or be devoted to somebody.

Love is a feeling, which exists in all men and women of the world. It is the feeling that generates a desire in the heart. "I love you" is a short phrase, but it is deeper than the ocean and higher than the sky.

To understand the depth of love, it is essential to understand what love is. Every man and woman has a different opinion about love. Each defines it according to his or her own family status, environment and capacity.

A well-known philosopher has said, "To love is equal to adore God." Love is the expression of happiness. Love is an actual meaning of life. In other words, without love, one cannot survive. Where there is love, there is continuity and expansion, and wherever there is selfishness, everything comes to an end.

An English poet says, "Love is always pleasant, whether one gives it or takes it." According to psychologist Albert Habbard, love is like a health tonic that supplies energy. Love is the power that lessens the distance between two hearts. Love brings interest in life. By falling in love, a person becomes polite, tender, cultured and sensitive, starts behaving like a poet and when the bud of love opens up, even a tyrant is compelled to surrender one's self to love.

The saying goes, "Love cannot be forced; it happens by itself." Several people in the world have shown true love by their life examples: Romeo-Juliet, Heer-Ranjha, Shirin-Farhad, Laila-Majnu to name a few among many in the pages of history. They made their love immortal. This world, which began with love betweeen Adam and Eve, will continue as long as there is love. When it disappears, it would be the end of the world.

There has been not much research on any other subject except love by researchers, psychologists, chemists and philosophers. One may wonder how many works of literature have been written on love? How many plays have been produced? And how many movies have been produced? But love remains a mystery, even after much research and study.

In the Indian context, love, passion and affection are not seen in good light. People disapprove of friendship and association with the opposite sex. Whatever opinion on love conservative people may have, the young generation is eager, keen and curious about love. They want to get themselves drowned in love.

The youth have found a new space through TV, movies, mobiles, media marketing, internet, etc. At the same time, they have forgotten the true meaning of "I love you" and have defined "free love" as a pretext to get closer for sex. The X-generation is lost in search of the destination of love. He or she feels the need for more information on love. It has become a necessity to understand the difference between love, friendship and free love.

Defining love as lust is not appropriate. It has to be corrected. Love remains sacred until it is free of sex. Love is lost when sex enters into the scene.

Love is an art. It is a skill. It has to be learnt like any other skill. The truth of the matter cannot be denied, but love needs to be studied.

Everybody must learn how to love and how to be loved. According to Catherine Anne Porter, love has to be learnt and learnt many times. There is no end to it. So love, fall in love and be loved.

In this book, the information on "how to love" is explained in detail as also the techniques on how to solve problems, the ups and downs of life, the joys and sorrows, trials and tribulations. If you want true love, pay attention to all aspects of this book. Follow them, step by step. Then discover for yourself how high, how deep and how sacred your love is.

2
Chemistry of Love

Love is the drop of the eyes that has been flowing for ages. When this drop turns into flood, it is difficult to stop it.

Love that sprouts in two hearts is the result of the chemicals produced in the brain. Why does one fall in love? How does love originate? Why do the hearts beat faster when a boy and a girl meet each other? Why do they start liking each other? Why can't they stay without each other? Scientists have done a thorough study on this subject and come out with several results.

According to scientific studies, there is a special kind of hormone in the body that stimulates love in a person. When lovers meet, a strange chemical reaction takes place. The image of an impressive personality is perceived by the brain and the message is then transmitted through the sensory nerves. As a result, a small ripple is created in the ocean of the heart. Then there is a slight pain in the heart. In other words, the heart gets impressed through the eyes. But scientists do not believe that love is nurtured in the heart. They say it is not the heart, but the brain where love is nurtured.

A psychologist from Britain, Michael Abent, says that there is a kind of hormone that brings about love between a male and a female. The hormone is produced in the brain. It is directly related to thoughts and emotions. Inside the mind, there is a bundle of minute capillaries collectively equal to the size of a pea. This is called the hypothalamus. It weighs almost quarter of an ounce. But it is very active even though it is so light. It brings harmony in all the physical and mental activities. At the same time, it controls and regulates the body temperature, blood pressure, appetite and thirst, fear, sleep, laughter, sex, etc. The hypothalamus is the factory where love originates.

The hormone 'oxytocin' present in the hypothalamus goes a long way in stimulating the emotions of love. According to Abent, it is not only oxytocin alone, but the whole chemical reaction that is involved in nurturing the emotion of love.

According to Dr Abent, this hormone gets affected at different levels. Oxytocin functions along with another hormone called prolactin. Famous scientist, Jack Packseth, says both these hormones produce 'opaedus' in the brain. The effect of this hormone is similar to that of sleep-stimulating drugs and intoxicating substances. That is why when people fall in love, they are said to be intoxicated with excitement. There is yet another hormone produced in the brain, which produces sweet and joyful emotions.

Dr Abent says in the newspaper *Guardian* published in London, that oxytocin is produced quickly in a friendly atmosphere.

He says strong light and high-tech machines hinder the flow of love. These elements exert pressure on the thought-receiving area called neo-cortex and so prevent the oxytocin from being released. As a result, the number of dedicated lovers is decreasing rapidly. Dr Abent also says that circumstances and environment have a lot of influence on devotion in love.

It depends on the genes whether to love truly or betray. Famous psychologist, Dr Anthony Walls has written in the most acclaimed book, *The Science of Love* that a fast chemical reaction occurs during the function and activities of bodily hormones. When emotions of love are produced in the brain, the pressure of norepinephrine and phenylethylene on the hypothalamus is increased. The hormone dopamine and norepinephrine produce emotions of happiness and joy while ethylene expresses love and affection. The moment these chemicals become active, it feels as if one is flying with the winds.

When love grows between a male and a female, the adrenaline hormone present in the pituitary gland is pressurised. As a result, the heart beat and the pulse rate increase. Pulse rate increases from 70 to 100. At this stage pressure on a chemical called endorphin begins to increase rapidly which spreads on the skin, giving a person a reddish or pinkish look. This increases physical beauty. That's why whenever a couple in love meets, there is a reddish glow and happiness spreads on their faces.

In Rowe University scientists have come to an understanding that boys and girls are attracted just because of the increased amount of dopamine in the brain. So girls are attracted faster to those boys who have a greater amount of dopamine.

Scientists from **birthpsychology.com** claim that the source of oxytocin is increased during the process of touching and embracing. It is at the highest level during intercourse and orgasm. Adrenaline is responsible for increasing the heart beats in girlfriends and boyfriends. Norpine and brain chemicals increase and excite the hearts. The function of these chemicals is to increase the heartbeat, excite and stimulate special organs and regularise all the reactions systematically.

The parts, where the signal originates and reaches different organs, become active. The signal which originates in the brain reaches different parts of the body and makes them active. Those who have experienced love also say that heart has a vital role to play in this precious moment, whereas scientists say that the role of the brain is greater than that of the heart.

How does the heart influence the brain? The scientists' answer to this question is that there are two parts of the brain that control the physical activities. One part controls the common thoughts, the other part controls emotions. When the amount of phenylethylene and dopamine increases, the portion of the brain that controls emotions becomes very active. As a result, the heart subdues the brain.

Psychologist Lorry Kistens of Texas Psychological University says that people often forget their meals when in love. This is due to increased flow of adrenaline that prevents the function of hunger for food. According to an American scientist, Dr Judith Wort, plenty of calories in the body are lost due to increased heartbeat and blood pressure, because of which couples in love are comparatively less obese than others.

The writer of *Boy We Love* and researcher, Hellen Fisher of Rotgers University claims that it is due to a change in the body of a lover that one loses appetite and patience. People in love are like mad people. This is due to a hormone called serotonin. This serotonin hormone keeps the tension away and the brain is kept calm and content.

In love, a person becomes blind. Scientist Robert Frayer has proved this. A special type of neuro-chemical, called phenylethylene prevents a person from noticing the weakness in his or her love.

Love for the opposite sex not only brings about alertness in the body but also a change in the internal activities. Psychologist Prof. Harry Race has clearly explained that those who live singly have a shorter life. Those who fall in love are physically and mentally sound and as a result they live longer.

Scientists are gradually unearthing the layers of love mystery. But lovers do not have anything to do with this mysterious information on love because it is only LOVE that they wish to know about, not the mysteries of love.

3

UR in Love

"Ishk par zor nahee hai, yeh woh aatish Galib ki
lagaye na lage, aur bujhaye na bhuje."

'Over love there is no control. It is that fire that no one can nake and nor can anyone put it out."

It cannot be predicted when and where one will fall in ɔve. Lovers enter the world of dreams. They start wandering n another world by riding on the winds of imagination as if heir contact or relation with this world is over. They start peaking to themselves. They feel a kind of magical change ɔithin themselves.

Chese are the symptoms of having fallen in love. If some of he following symptoms are present in you, then consider ou are in love.

- You are lost in your thoughts. You avoid meeting people; you talk less. This is love.
- You feel a kind of restlessness. You feel something is missing, in spite of having everything; then you are in love.

- You smile to yourself when you think about certain things, then you are in love.
- When you feel like talking to yourself, then consider yourself in love.
- You stumble while walking on the plain road and you slip on your way; then consider you are in love.
- You stagger while walking and you count your steps while walking; then consider you are in love.
- You feel a wave of happiness in your body the moment you hear his or her name; then consider you are in love.
- When you feel her or him as soon as you close the eyes and you cannot sleep at night, then consider you are in love.
- When you want to say so many things and your lips are sealed, then consider you are in love.
- When your eyes become moist while laughing, then consider you are in love.
- When you relate everything to her or him, then consider you are in love.
- When you spend hours in waiting for her or him by standing on the terrace, the balcony or anywhere else, just hoping that she or he might pass by and you will have an eye-to-eye contact, then consider you are in love.

- When you start liking even childish and ridiculous acts of his or hers, then consider you are in love.
- All of a sudden you start adoring God. You start visiting temples or become religious and start repeating the names of gods, then consider you are in love.
- When emotions of kindness and generosity get stimulated in you and you begin to feel good on helping others, then consider you are in love.
- When reading books bores you and you start humming love songs, then consider you are in love.
- When someone comes into your dream and casts magical spells on you, then consider you are in love.
- When you become anxious and swoon and dance whenever romantic songs are played on TV, FM, tape, etc., then consider you are in love.
- When you feel good about the experience of first showers in the rainy season while others dislike it, then consider you are in love.
- When you get thrilled for every small act of hers or his or your heart starts crying, or you start sulking, then consider you are in love.
- When something happens as soon as her or his thoughts come to your mind, then consider you are in love.
- When you start getting carried away with happiness and feel like singing romantic songs , then consider you are in love.

- When you perpetually feel like seeing him or her or you look forward to seeing him or her, then consider you are in love.
- When you feel like saying something before he or she comes and you are unable to say anything when the person comes. And your lips remain fluttering, then consider you are in love.
- When you feel like showing him or her the things you buy, then consider you are in love.
- When you have a kind of strange tingle when you see him or her and you are in the seventh heaven on meeting him or her, then consider you are in love.
- When you look into the mirror very often and when you get agitated by a small blemish on your face, then consider you are in love.
- When you give extra care on your looks and personality and when you begin to seek professional advice for it, then consider you are in love.
- When you change your hairstyle and seek advice of your friends, then consider you are in love.
- If you lose weight without dieting, then consider you are in love.

- When you acquire an amazing dress sense and feel like changing dress every hour, or when you feel like wearing or buying a new dress every day, then consider you are in love.
- When you forget about your likes and dislikes and you give more importance to his or her likes and dislikes, then consider you are in love.
- When you like everything of his or hers, then consider you are in love.
- When you go crazy about every behaviour of his or hers, then consider you are in love.
- When you become intoxicated even with his or her bad smell, then consider you are in love.
- When you feel like meeting him or her alone instead of meeting him or her with friends, then consider you are in love.
- When you feel like dying for him or her, then consider you are in love.
- When you start using more 'we' than 'I' , then consider you are in love.
- When you start being engrossed in romantic imagination and imagine he or she is in your arms and you lie down by putting your head on his or her lap, then consider you are in love.

- When you begin to feel nobody is as beautiful or handsome as she or he is, then consider you are in love.
- If one day he or she is not seen, you feel wretched thoughts, coming to your mind and you become very nervous and start praying to God for his or her safety, then consider you are in love.
- When he or she goes out of the city, you worry about him or her, then consider you are in love.
- When life starts seeming boring, nonsensical, stupid and incomplete without him or her, then consider you are in love.
- When you forget the world and remember only his or her words, then consider you are in love.
- When you dial his or her number first before calling anybody else, then consider that you are in love.
- When you begin to imagine yourself to be the hero and she the heroine, or vice versa, then consider you are in love.
- When you begin to lose appetite and you don't remember to eat your meal, then consider you are in love.
- When you have no peace of mind in the day and no sleep at night, then consider you are in love.
- When you start wearing clothes that match his or her clothes, then consider you are in love.

- When you begin to read about fashion, fitness, beauty tips, my first love, love tips, etc. in newspapers and magazines and avoid reading about social, political events and about career, then consider you are in love.
- When you read his or her stars first in newspapers and when you remain sad the whole day if anything unfavourable is predicted, then consider you are in love.
- When you forget your date of birth but you always remember the date of birth of his or her as well as the family members, then consider you are in love.
- When you start paying attention to *ghazals* or sad songs, start suggesting that he or she hear such songs, give long lectures on *sher-o-shairi* as if you are an expert on that, then consider you are in love.
- When you think you have magical powers and start assuming that you can disappear and you can go from one place to another, then consider you are in love.
- When you find everything of his or her to be nice, then consider you are in love.
- When you don't bother to change dress at night and go to bed without taking off your jeans and T-shirt, then consider you are in love.
- When you imagine yourself to be nude while you see scantily dressed girls or boys in newspaper advertisements, then consider you are in love.

- When you start window-shopping of male or female items, then consider you are in love.
- When you keep the password of his or her name as a code, then consider you are in love.
- When your eyes begin to follow him or her whenever he or she goes away to the toilet or anywhere else, then consider you are in love.
- When you feel like kissing him or her pet dog or cat, then consider you are in love.
- When you feel like taking plenty of photographs of his or her, then consider you are in love.
- When he or she talks to some other boy or girl, you begin to feel jealous and feel like killing him or her by strangling him or her, then consider you are in love.

4

How to Know Someone Loves You?

One can have the awareness of love at any time. But some people cannot understand the feelings of others from their behaviour and attitude. When he or she goes away, only then a person realises that he or she likes him or her. Given below are some clues that will help you find whether someone likes you or not.

- If his or her eyes always look for you, then know he or she likes you.
- Whenever he or she meets you and always praises you and only you, then know he or she likes you.
- If he or she blushes upon seeing you and becomes cheerful, then know that he or she likes you.
- If he or she stops you from lifting heavy items and does not allow you to do risky things, then know that he or she likes you.
- If he or she is ready to go anywhere you want to take, then know that he or she likes you.

- If he or she asks you to take him or her around whenever you both meet, then know that he or she likes you.
- If he or she chooses to sit in a corner when you take him or her to a park, then know that he or she likes you.
- If he or she never forgets to say goodnight by calling you on your mobile before going to bed, then know that he or she likes you.
- If he or she makes all your likes as his or her likes, then know that he or she likes you.
- If he or she insists that you teach him or her to drive a two-wheeler or car, then know that he or she likes you.
- If he or she knows what you like to eat and what you don't, then know that he or she likes you.
- If he or she compares you to some film star, then know that he or she likes you.
- If his or her eyes always follow you, then know that he or she likes you.
- If he or she keeps your birthday in mind, then he or she likes you.
- If he or she happens to be the first to wish you, then know that he or she likes you.
- If he or she takes your advice to buy even the small items, then know that he or she likes you.

- If he or she insists you go to shop with him or her, then know that he or she likes you.
- If you happen to be the first one to tells the news of his or her success, then know that he or she likes you.
- If he or she sends messages frequently on your mobile, then know that he or she likes you.

5

How to Propose to Someone

Filmstar Ashok Kumar, alias Dadamoni fell in love with a beautiful heroine, Devika Rani. But he was not able to express his love to her. One day he said to Montu, the storywriter, "Devika Rani is rooted in my heart. But what do I do? I don't have the courage to express my love to her."

This happens to every lover. Although it is difficult to express one's love, it is not impossible. There are some tips given below on how to express love. You can try any of the tips. You can even find out some more tips yourself.

- You can send a proposal or a greeting card to express your love.
- You can write a lovely message on a beautiful, colourful paper and send it across to him or her.
- You can write a love letter. This is quite an old method, but it is as popular today as it was before.
- You could send sweets. If the sweet is in the shape of a heart, then love expressed will feel sweeter.

- You can express your love by giving romantic books, novels, etc.
- You could express love by presenting him or her a Walkman with FM.
- You can present him or her a music system for the car and express your love.
- By signing an autograph or taking his or her autograph first, you can express love.
- You can express your love by offering a lift on your motorbike or car.
- Each person can be different in expressing his or her love. Poets can express love through their poems; storywriters through their stories; lyricists through their lyrics.
- If you are an artist, you can express your love by drawing his or her portrait.
- Music lovers can express their love by presenting a new music composition.
- A lover can express his or her love by publishing a message in the newspaper.
- You can present a mobile phone and express your love for him or her by sending SMS.
- By having the first letter of his or her name written on some personal items like a ring, chain, top and any other jewellery, you can express your love.

- You can express your love by sending a bouquet of roses or other flowers (for more information read chapter on Flower Messages).
- You can even send an e-mail to express that you have fallen in love with him or her.
- You could express your love to a girl by wishing Valentine's Day at midnight on the 13th of Feb.
- You can express your love by inviting him or her to be your partner for the 'Best Valentine Couple' competition.
- You can express your love by inviting him or her to dance in a bar, discotheque or a poolside.
- You can also express your love by shaking hands or by kissing him or her.
- By taking him or her for a long drive or by making a plan to roam around nearby is also a way of expressing one's love.
- You can express your love by getting your message publicised through FM or TV channels.
- You can get your love expressed by publishing the Valentine Day message in special columns set aside for that day.
- You can express your love by presenting a diary, table calendar, wall calendar, etc. with love quotations.
- You can invite him or her to a candlelight dinner at some

hotel or restaurant and let him or her know that you love him or her.

- You can express your love by throwing a party or by organising some other function at your place.
- At the party, hang a balloon filled with petals and spangles against the ceiling. Take your boyfriend or girlfriend under the balloon and burst the balloon. He or she will be showered with the petals and spangles and this new way of expressing love will excite your partner.
- You can take a hoarding on hire and have his or her name and proposal printed so that he or she can read it while passing by.
- You can make use of 'fume bomb' in order to express your love. The name of your boyfriend or girlfriend will be written in the colourful smoke when the bomb is set to explode.

Make use of new words in order to express your love

- I have saved your name in the hard disk of my heart.
- The ring tone of your name is ringing in my heart.
- My heart beeps on seeing you, otherwise it would remain locked.
- How many times I have sent, 'I Love You' in my name? See in the message box of your heart.

6
Style of Proposing

To understand a heart it requires a lifetime.
Girls do not open up in just four days of courtship.

Do not propose to a boy or a girl in film-style. According to Geb Fishburg, the writer of 'Guide to Picking Girls', *you should talk to yourself before you propose to any boy or girl. Think whether you are fit for him or her. Does he or she like you? What would you feel if he or she rejects? Would you be able to bear the pain of rejection? Do some homework for this. It will help you understand how to propose and the reaction you will receive after that.*

- Speak your first sentences confidently. Do not stammer or hesitate. Neither girls nor boys like those who stammer and hesitate.
- Propose to the boy or girl you like face to face. Do not propose to him or her behind the back or by calling out from behind or by taking him or her by surprise. Girls and boys do not consider this to be nice.

- Use words which represent the voice of your heart. Do not make use of pompous words in order to impress. This would seem artificial and stupid.
- If a suitable phrase is not coming to your mind, just say 'How are you?' to start the conversation. Although such phrases do not express your love, you can at least break the ice and get friendly with the friend.
- If the boy or girl you are proposing to is younger or older than you, try to know him or her better, for example, find out what he or she does. How long he or she has been working? What are his or her hobbies? Who all are in the family? Analyse after having all the information and ask yourself whether the friend is suitable for you.
- Never compliment yourself. Do not pretend to be smart.
- Compliment him or her for her beauty but do not compare him or her with others, like, 'You look exactly like Aishwarya', or 'You look like Dilip Kumar!' From such things he or she will infer that you are not crazy about him or her but about his or her body and that you are only interested in sex.
- When you start a conversation with a boy or girl, always speak gently and politely. You will have an incomplete feeling about you if you speak fast or rush without giving enough details. He or she will be disappointed in you.
- Keep your cool while having a conversation. Do not

get carried away and start speaking on hot topics in the first meeting. He or she will feel insecure with you.

- Do not speak about sex in the initial period. If you do so, you may be considered rude and brazen.
- There is a likelihood of your becoming successful if you propose in a correct manner. The style of proposing should be such that he or she becomes yours, for sure.

Take care of the following points

- Never propose by using wrong, dirty, rude and filthy words.
- Do not overact while expressing your love.
- Do not tease and make fun of him or her in order to express your love.
- Never express your love by showing off.
- Adopt polite ways to express your love.
- It does not seem proper if one whistles or pushes in order to express love.
- Do not beat about the bush to express your feelings. Be straightforward in what you have to say.
- Do not take the help of your friends in order to express your love.

7
How to Select a Friend

Girls are very choosy about selecting their boyfriends and same is the case with boys. They take a lot of precautions about it. They select only those who pass the test of love. So boys and girls should be careful in selecting their friends. It is not easy to select a friend. You need to do full planning. It should not be that whosoever you meet, you make him or her your friend. If you select your friend in a rush, you might get into big trouble later on.

Before selecting

- Before selecting a friend, study about him or her completely.
- Try to understand the body language of the girl or the boy before making your friend.
- Don't just consider the overt beauty and go crazy and propose to him or her. Judge her or his nature and attitude.

- Girls take a long time to open up. Only after that, one gets to know about her character and personality. Boys are easier to become friends with.
- Propose to him or her only after you are fully satisfied.
- If a girl has proposed to you, then take the decision only after investigating thoroughly. Same is the case with the girl.
- Though the saying goes, 'There is no rich or poor in love', forget about it, because it is far better to make a friend of your own status, than to be unsuccessful later.
- Collect the details of his or her family before making him or her your friend.
- Find about his or her friend circle before making him or her your friend. By doing so you will know a lot about the person's nature and character.
- Find out about his or her hobbies and state of mind. If hobbies do not correspond, then thoughts will not match either.
- Avoid boys or girls who go on making several friends.
- Do not rush in when choosing your boyfriend or girlfriend. Go step by step. Judge well and then accept the friend.
- Check if the boy or girl is not pretending to be in love with you. You might suffer a heartbreak if you come to know the truth. You may have to shed tears of blood.

- Don't make him or her your friend if somebody proposes on the streets, because even callgirls propose to good-looking gentleman. They rob you of your prestige and transmit many deadly diseases. Same holds true for girls who should not have many male friends.
- Don't make one your friend, who just complies to please you, because the day he or she disagrees about anything, you will feel bad about it.
- It is better to avoid a cunning or an item girl or boy.
- The person suitable to be your friend would be one who loves you; not the one who is after your money.
- The boy or girl, who seems to be smart, bold, modern and dynamic does not prove to be a good friend.
- The boy or girl who starts talking about sex after a few meetings, sends sexy MMS or SMS, likes to watch romantic or sexy movies, or likes to go to porn-sites, is not of a good character. Stay away from such a person.

Make a list

- Make a complete list of your bad habits and weaknesses.
- Make a list of those qualities that you would like to see in your friend.

Think about it yourself

- If you cannot change yourself, then change the list that contains the qualities of your friend.
- Try to judge yourself by placing both the lists and ask yourself whether you are really eligible for the friend you are looking for. If you are not, then try to change yourself.
- Select a friend of your status. If you are from a rich family, then make a friend of the same status, because a boy or girl coming from a status lower than you will not be able to maintain all that well. Later on you will have to repent.
- The first quality that a boy wants in a girl is her beauty and same is true in the boy. Even a beautiful girl would like a lot of good qualities in her boyfriend. Same is true of a boy. That is why inculcate good qualities in yourself and not the bad ones.
- Give more importance to good qualities rather than beauty. According to psychologists, good qualities will eventually prove to be ideal.

A confident step

- Do not rush in selecting your friend. Anything done in a hurry may prove to be wrong as well.
- Take the decision only after repeatedly weighing the pros and cons of your thoughts.
- Do not select your friend by compromising on anything.

Four points

- Sometimes there may be objections to your love.
- There is no such thing as first, second or third love. Love is only love.
- In love, the burden of favours may bend life sometimes.
- Before falling in love, make sure that the fragrance of the deodorant or body odour of the boy or girl does not turn you off.

8
Types of Proposals

Psychologists have made an intensive study about the different styles of proposing. One of the psychologists is Prof. Domarik, who has classified the style into four categories. This can be understood from the way they eat.

Long Luncher : The boy or girl who finishes his or her meal very slowly, can be understood that he or she will propose after a long time. This could be beyond what you can tolerate.

What you can do : You must take the initiative to express your love for him or her.

Wild Woofer : The boy or girl who finishes lunch fast will propose to you very soon.

What you can do : Accept the proposal immediately.

Plate Fisher : The boy or girl who plays with the food displayed on the plate and remains lost in thoughts while eating will take a long time to propose. Such boys or girls are only physically present with you. They are mentally absent.

What you can do: Try to bring him or her on the right track.

Secret Scroffer : The boy or girl who insists on having lunch at a quiet, lonely place, and wants to sit at a corner, then consider that he or she likes you very much, but he or she hesitates to propose.

What you can do: Remove the hesitation so that he or she can propose or you can take the initiative to propose.

2 points

- If you like the boy or girl and realise that he or she is crazy about you, then do not take long to propose. Do it immediately.
- Do not express your love in a film style. He or she will consider you a flirt or a deceiver.

9

Love at First Sight

It happens often that you like a boy or girl at first sight and you consider him or her to be everything for you. You start reacting, "Wow! How beautiful she was. She killed me at first sight and she has robbed me off my sleep," or "How handsome he is. I fell for him." According to psychologists, there is no such thing as love at first sight.

It is just a feeling. It is a game of hormones. It increases the heartbeat. It stimulates them. Those people who do not get carried away and take steps patiently, their love becomes immortal. It does not remain like a four-day fever, but instead their love becomes an ideal love.

Those youngsters, who get carried away as the strings of their heart start vibrating and their entire body gets heated up, start behaving like roadside Romeos or Juliets.

Such reactions can be seen in boys and girls. Girls can be turned on when they see a smart builder, city-

smart-dandy or a different type of person. They don't usually react immediately. They can control their excitement. But boys are unable to do so. So excitement can be seen in their behaviour.

Love at first sight is often seen because of sexual attraction. Boys and girls consider this sexual attraction to be true love. Actually it is not called love but just an attraction, which normally happens between the opposite sex. When two persons of opposite sex stay close for a long time, they wrongly presume that they are in love.

- ❤ When you seem to fall in love with anyone, get to know him or her fully to confirm it is not just an infatuation.
- ❤ Find out after three or four meetings whether he or she is suitable for you or not.
- ❤ Don't trust anyone at first sight. Often the boy or girl, who eventually deceives, pretends to be very cultured. So do not give your heart to one without getting to know him or her fully.
- ❤ Don't make those boys or girls your ideal who seem to be rich, glamorous and own cars. Nowadays boys and girls make use of this formula to trap the opposite sex.
- ❤ Smart looking girls fulfil their wishes by trapping smart boys and vice versa. So beware of these types.
- ❤ It is foolishness to give your heart to somebody at first sight.

- Sometimes boys fall for married women who look like unmarried girls. They get obsessed with them and when they come to know the truth, they repent.
- Nowadays the trend of trapping young boys by married women has gained currency. These women fulfil their sexual urge by trapping naive boys. They discard them like rubbish after making use of them.
- Don't be serious at first sight. Make sure that you are not going to repent when you give your heart in a hurry.

10

Which Young-One Looks Sexy

Smart or handsome is being termed sexy. What are the qualities that make a man sexy? Let's see how boys seem sexy to girls.

- Boys using phrases like 'please', 'thank you', 'sorry' are considered sexy by girls.
- Boys who cover their mouth when they yawn and say 'excuse me' when they cough or sneeze seem sexy to girls.
- Boys who have excellent dress sense and are aware of their body language seem sexy to girls.
- Boys who drive carefully at a reasonable speed seem sexy to girls.
- Boys interested in music, art and literature seem sexy to girls.
- Boys, who are able to argue about any subject, seem sexy to girls.
- Boys, who are punctual for meetings, make calls on time and are dedicated to their work seem sexy to girls.

- Boys having presence of mind and sense of humour seem sexy to girls.
- Boys, who are eager to help others and eager to share jokes seem sexy to girls.
- Boys, who love pet animals, talk about flowers and love natural things are considered sexy by girls.
- Girls consider boys who leave their seats to ladies while travelling by a train or bus, and are ready to solve any problems faced by them, sexy.
- Boys, who compliment girls for their beauty and figure, seem sexy to girls.

11

Judge and then Go Ahead

Before falling in love with anyone, judge him or her completely, else you won't get anything except repentance.

- Judge if your friend is interested in your wealth rather than you.
- Nowadays girls keep more than one boyfriend at a time and vice versa. So it is advisable to make a thorough investigation about the boy or girl.
- See if the boy or girl is immature or childish which could be the reason why he or she may fall in love with you.
- See if he or she praises another boy or girl in front of you. It means she loves you. At the same time, the praise of another boy or girl means he or she loves him or her as well.
- Judge if your friend refuses to say anything about his or her family.
- Judge if he or she throws tantrums when you are late but when he or she is late himself or herself, does not even say sorry.

- See if he or she repeatedly talks against love and considers that he or she does not have any emotions of love in him or her.
- Judge if he or she does not have words to say about love.
- See whether he or she is not at all sensitive about your love.
- See if he or she is only interested in blowing your money for fun.

12

See that you don't have to Repent

If you want to see your love reach the ultimate end, that is, marriage, then make sure you do not tell lies to your friend. If you do it, you may have to repent. If he or she comes to know the truth, he or she will suffer a heartbreak. A heart once broken cannot be mended. Even if it is joined, the crack will remain.

Love is like a thread of silk. It does not break so easily but once it breaks, a knot forms if you try to join the two parts. And the knot is not that strong. It can break again if there is a little stretch or tension. So never tell stories or lies to your friend.

- Tell the truth about your family. Do not exaggerate to show false pride.
- Give correct information about your job and income.
- Do not spend a lot of money to show off.
- Do not give expensive gifts to your friend, boy or girl.

- ❤ Cut your coat according to your cloth. Do not show off by borrowing money from your friends.
- ❤ If you are riding a bike, don't talk about a car.

Attention!

- ❍ Don't reveal dubious dealings or actions in front of your friend.
- ❍ Keep your fantasies to yourself. Don't reveal them.
- ❍ Don't tell your friend that you are not happy with your job or life.
- ❍ Don't try to assure your love by making a promise or taking an oath.
- ❍ Don't call your friend at midnight, no matter how anxious you are.
- ❍ Don't seek his or her advice for every little incident in your personal life.
- ❍ Don't introduce him or her to every friend or relative of yours.
- ❍ Don't indulge in give and take or borrowing and lending with your friend.
- ❍ If you love him or her very much, don't use the same words repeatedly to express your love. Instead, show it with your behaviour and attitude.

- Don't make use of 'sorry' or 'thank you' too much. It would sound too formal to both of you.
- Don't pressurise your friend to do any job or take up any course.
- Don't try to thrust your likes and dislikes on your friend.

13

Love and Lust

The names of Laila-Majnu, Romeo-Juliet, Heer-Ranjha, Shirin-Farhad and several others have been written umpteen number of times in stories of immortal love. If you too, wish to make your love story immortal, then try to know the difference between love and lust.

In the Oxford Dictionary, *love is defined as attraction towards the opposite sex; a spiritual bond with somebody while lust is defined as a desire for sex and gratification.*

According to psychologists, love keeps on increasing whereas lust ends as soon as it starts. There are some examples given below. You can see for yourself whether you are in love or a victin of lust.

Love is

- Talking about tender feelings.
- Praising good qualities.
- Demonstrated by touch.

- Presenting a gift.
- Sending good SMSes.
- Sending ring tones and wallpaper.
- Showing respect for your friend.

Lust is

- Talking about sexuality.
- Complimenting on different parts of the body.
- Trying to cuddle or stick close to your friend.
- Presenting porno books, blue films and CDs.
- Sending sexy clips.
- Talking about running away from home.

14

'Crush' Lovers

During teenage, if a boy or girl secretly looks out of the window and forgets to have the meals, sleep, wake up, studies, remains detached, and is always looking for somebody, then consider that he or she is a victim of 'crush'. All these are symptoms of having a 'crush' on somebody.

A victim of 'crush' does not come in front in order to please the person he or she loves. He or she writes letters but reads them to himself or herself and then tears it; or types e-mails, but instead of sending them, he or she deletes them.

According to psychologists, a teenager may have a crush on anybody. He or she starts loving a boy or girl either much too older than him or her or much too younger to him or her. Sometimes he or she even begins to love his or her class/school teacher. He or she writes love letters but does not send them.

A 'crush' lover can be called as a kind of one-sided lover. A one-sided lover tends to be crazy. He or she can do anything in order to achieve his or her love, but 'crush' lovers do not express their love at all.

Things to do for a crush lover

- Don't have the desire to fall in love with aged men or girls. Fall in love with a boy or girl of your age.
- Instead of loving someone in your mind, try to propose to him or her. Perhaps you'd be lucky to have his or her love.
- Give information about the boy or girl you admire to your friends. It may so happen that he or she will come to know about your love through them.
- Don't give up studying for the sake of love. First give priority to education and career and then love.
- If the 'crush' increases in intensity, you may become a victim of madness. Start taking care of yourself before it.

15
Are You Obsessed with Sex?

What is love? Scientists, sociologists, psychologists and philosophers have defined love differently. Despite so many studies on love, it is said that no one has been able to give the most acceptable definition of love up till today. Every lover takes love in his or her own way. It has become common to consider love as sex. What do you think of love? Is it love or sex?

Check for yourself whether

- You try to catch, hold, embrace or kiss your friend as soon as you see him or her.
- You try to fix your eyes to see underneath his or her clothes.
- You talk about going to a lonely place when you meet him or her.
- You watch porn videos and CDs.
- You try to excite him or her by holding or touching his or her body parts.

- You give him or her romantic and sexy books to read.
- You present him or her sexy outfits.
- You eventually end up talking about sex indirectly.
- You send sexy SMS or MMS messages.
- You don't have objection to having sex before marriage.

If you say YES to the above statements, then it means you do not love your friend. You only have the desire to have sex with him or her. You are obsessed with sex.

If you say half YES and half NO, then you love him or her, but you want to have sex as well. So you must try to improve yourself.

If you say NO, then you are an ideal lover. Your friend will be proud of you.

16
All is not Fair in Love

It is said that 'all is fair in love and war'. In other words, one should win by hook or by crook. But this does not seem valid for love, because you cannot achieve someone's love by force. Many lovers adopt unfair means to obtain love. Do not use wrong methods to win your love. Adopt only fair methods to gain true love.

Many boys try to impress girls in the film style. First, they tease or make fun of their friend or hire some bullies. Then they try to become valiant by fighting with them on the spot.

Many boys pretend to be rich. They borrow money from their friends in order to impress their girlfriends. They even do not hesitate to steal money from home.

Several boys trap naive girls by their smooth talk and persuade them to run away from home. They have fun with the money stolen from home and with the jewellery of their girlfriend. After the money is finished, they get rid of them.

Many boys have one-sided love with the girls. They merely pretend their love just as Shahrukh Khan did in the movie called *'Darr'*.

Many boys lay a snare for the girlfriends of other friends to attract them. For this they even create misunderstandings between them.

There are some boys who get so mad in one-sided love that they kidnap the girl and force her to marry. If she refuses, they even kill her.

If you want to win your girlfriend by adopting any of the above methods, then you are wrong. All these techniques are not fair in true love.

Actually love cannot be forced. Make sacrifices in love. Don't be arrogant at all, because love wants sacrifice, not force.

The same is true for girls who should not try to win their boyfriend's love through force or coercion.

If you want to obtain somebody's love, then propose to his or her gently and hope to win his or her love. To be in search of love is beautiful, but to find love without searching is even more beautiful.

17
Dating and Style

You must cast a good impression if you want to be a success. For this, you must pay special attention to your style. Style means your body language, dressing, confidence, etc. should be such that you make a good impression on the boy or girl.

As the saying goes, 'first impression is the last impression,' remember to

- Be ready with some special expressions.
- Have your hair set several days earlier. If you want to change your hairstyle, do it weeks prior to the dating.
- Get yourself shaved before going. If you have a beard, have the setting done.
- Have a bath before going on a date. Use a good quality deodorant to get rid of bad smell. Use a strong perfume before leaving.
- Use a special kind of dating perfume.

- Make sure that you don't waste time on shopping on the day of dating.
- If you want to buy anything new, do it at least a few days in advance.
- Keep your mood fresh on that day. Forget about all your worries. Go ahead on your date with happiness and enthusiasm.
- Reach on time. It is a sign of negligence to be late on a first date.
- Don't ask about your style when you meet your boyfriend or girlfriend. He or she will comment on your style himself or herself.
- Compliment your friend's dress sense, style and makeup.
- If your mouth has bad breath, do not panic. Take chewing gum, mouth freshener or mouth spray, etc.

18

Dating and Power Dressing

When you go on a date it is essential that you know how to dress or wear proper clothes. You must select your dress according to your body type. According to personality experts, youth, according to their body types, can be classified into three types. First, those who have broader shoulders than hips; second, those who have broader hips than shoulders; third, those who have the same sized shoulders and hips.

- Keep your own style and look.
- Copy some ideal style. Don't imitate just any style.
- Wear designer dresses. They would make you look impressive.You could copy some celebrities' outfits if you want.
- If you are imitating anybody, make sure that the dress suits your body and looks perfect on you.
- The design, cut and style of your dress should be such that it adds to your personality.

- Take care of the accessories along with your dress: tie, socks, shoes, belt, spectacles, etc. or long dress, sandals, bag, etc. should be according to your dress.
- Your dress should neither be too tight, nor too loose. It should be comfortable to wear.
- It would look attractive if you choose your dress according to your stature.
- Avoid out-of-date and old-fashioned dresses.
- Try putting on a new dress to see if it is not uncomfortable.
- Pay attention to your colour choice. See the matching and contrast colours of your dress. Just as the fashion changes, some colours also gain currency with changing times. Sometimes light and sometimes dark colours happen to be in fashion.
- If you have less broad shoulders, wear boat-necked shirts only. The lapel of the coat should be thick and it should be outward. The pockets of your pants should be crossed. It is better if you wear pants without pleats.
- Those who have the same sized shoulders and hips, they can wear any type of dress.
- If you have broad shoulders, wear a shirt with short sleeves. The lapels of the coat should be thin and low.
- If you have short legs, wear your pants a little above your hips so that the legs appear longer. The coat should be of normal size with three buttons.

- Skinny youth should wear double-breasted coats and thick, striped or checked shirts.
- If you have a tall figure, you should wear light coloured pants and a dark coloured shirt.
- Do wear your belt if you have a tall figure. It will help you look less tall as the body will be divided into two parts.
- Those who have fat and heavy bodies, they look better in sack-suits.
- Those who have normal body, they look good only in American style suits.
- Slim persons look good in English-style suits.
- Ties come in different colours and designs. You can match your tie with your shirt and wear it.
- Wear dark dresses at night and light coloured dresses during the day.
- A girl should wear the right dress and sandals to match with the dress and the handbag.
- A short girl should wear long dresses without a break in the middle. Tall girls can wear two-piece outfits.
- Learn to follow the fashion that suits you as a girl.

19

Don't do like This

Many youth and girls misunderstand the meaning of dating. They think that if the girl or boy has come for dating, they can have physical contacts. Do not associate dating with sex. Dating is meant for understanding and judging each other. Pay attention to your personality when you are on a date. Even a small mistake may drive your friend away from you.

- Do not force your friend to have a physical relationship.
- Do not insist if he or she refuses.
- Choose a public place or where there is a ticket system for dating.
- Try to know about each other's hobbies and interests.
- Do not go to a deserted place for dating.
- It is not advisable to speak loudly, burst into laughter, talk about sexual items, narrate sexy and raunchy jokes and boast too much. Talk gently and politely.
- Do not make your friend tense by telling about your problems.

- If your friend is anxious or worried, try your best to solve his or her problem.
- Don't give expensive gifts during the starting days of dating.
- Do not talk about anything that might put mental pressure on your friend.
- Do not talk ambiguously and do speak indirectly.
- Be confident, but do not be overconfident.
- Present yourself with your best sex appeal.

What not to say

- Never say to your friend that Aishwarya is cute and you want to hug her or that Amitabh Bachchan is handsome.
- He or she looks like a monkey in his or her new hairstyle.
- When he or she sings in a romantic mood, do not say that he or she sings off-tune.
- You feel like singing on a date with other girls or boys.
- That your friend has an ego problem.
- How caring and emotional the other girl or boy is!
- He or she sits awkwardly on the bike.
- The perfume or deodorant he or she has used is of low quality.

- People in office find him or her very strange.
- He or she is irritating, stubborn, talkative and over-smart.
- Many boys or girls have proposed to you before.
- Even now many boys or girls propose to you.
- You are very different from the boy or girl you like.
- His or her family never liked him or her.
- Friends like you are suitable just for timepass.
- He or she feels jealous on speaking to other boys or girls.
- He or she was happier with his ex-friend.
- Even now he or she misses his ex-friend.
- You are dull in front of his or her ex-friend.
- You don't know how to apply make-up or to dress properly. Your hairstyle does not suit you at all.
- You don't have any dress sense and the colour choice is atrocious.
- Your manner of speaking is rude, sexy or like that of Lalita Pawar.
- You wink flirtatiously as if you are hinting to go to bed.
- You look like an ostrich in high heels or a three-piece suit.
- You move your hand as if you are a callgirl or a man of loose character.
- Thank God, I fell in love with you, otherwise, who would have cared for you?

20

Measure the Depth of Love

There is no measuring cup to measure the depth of love, so that you can know how much somebody loves you. Lovers find out the depth of love without any measuring cup. There are certain times, which indicate the depth of love. By paying attention to the things given below you can measure the depth of your love.

Fail to keep promises: If your friend does not reach the decided venue on time, consider that there is no depth in his or her love.

Praises others: If he or she goes on to praise other friends instead of praising you, then he or she does not love you so much.

Lost in thoughts: If he or she is present physically for the sake of formality and is mentally absent whenever you meet him or her, or does not pay attention to you and is lost in thoughts somewhere, then consider that there is a big pit in between you and him or her.

Not making calls: Lovers always like to remain in the ocean of love. So they talk for hours on the phone whenever they are apart. Even after this, they are not satisfied. If your friend does not call you when he or she is away and does not say much after saying 'Hi' or 'Hello' and disconnects the phone, then consider that he or she does not have anything to do with your love.

Not being excited: If your friend remains cold and sad whenever you meet him or her, then consider that he or she is not interested in you.

Avoiding to meet: If your friend avoids meeting you when you ask him or her out and he or she makes excuses about being busy with studies or some other important job, then consider that he or she does not want to meet you.

Wanting to go back: Lovers do not think of separating from each other when they meet. If your friend wants to return immediately after you meet him or her, then it is certain that he or she does not love you.

21
Girlfiend or Boyfriend Means.....

Gone are the times when it was difficult to make girlfriends or boyfriends. Today it is easy to do so. But it is difficult to find a right friend. With the changing times, the meaning of the words have changed. Let's see where you will find your girlfriend or boyfriend in these new words:

Generation X - who was born between 1965–1977.

Generation Y - who was born after 1978.

Generation D - who uses digital gadgets.

Generation nex - from the story of the next generation.

Generation XL - what is this? (fat like Tuntun)

Generation XLL - ugh! Oh my God! (fatter than Tuntun).

Generation netizen - (internet + citizen) who spends most of his or her time on the internet.

Generation CAD - (ctrl+Alt+Del) seeing old issues in a new light.

Puppy leave - who bunks office or college and spends most of his or her time with pet dog.

Bett call - making calls from your mobile.

Mucus trooper - one who goes to office or college, even if he or she has a cold.

Himbo - who is best to look at but is cool by nature.

Affluenza - (affluence + influenza) who is too materialistic and borrows money from friends to buy new things.

Restrosexual - one who never pays attention to style, dress sense and personality.

Leather spinster - who does not want to get married and says that he or she is fine as he or she is.

Cell yell - who talks loudly on mobile phones.

Toxic - who is selfish and unkind.

22

Manners of Your Girlfriend or Boyfriend that make You go Crazy

Normally every youth and girl finds everything of his girlfriend or boyfriend to be nice. But certain gestures or manners make you go crazy about him or her.

- His or her mischief, her restlessness, her flirtatious behaviour and mannerism.
- His or her smile seems as if raindrops are falling in the rainy season.
- His or her voice makes your heart vibrate.
- His or her twisting and stretching of limbs makes you crazy.
- The way he or she speaks freely makes your heart beat faster.
- Your heart gets agitated when he or she winks at you or gazes at you.
- His or her fashionable dress makes you say koo.. koo..

- His or her way of doing make-up or dressing is really attractive.
- His or her looking at you in the crowd with half-closed eyes increases your heartbeat.
- The way he or she is embarrassed upon proposing to him or her and the way he or she cuddles you and you feel good by merely thinking about it.
- Singing romantic songs while going on a long drive and you wishing that the time would never pass by.
- His or her becoming happy at every gesture of yours makes you crazy.
- Sitting quietly with his or her eyes upon your eyes makes you intoxicated.
- You wish that the time would stop when he or she places his or her head on your shoulders and speaks about love.
- You feel like humming instead of getting angry when he or she scolds, shouts and gets offended.
- The closer he or she gets the farther it seems. The farther he or she goes away the more you miss him or her.
- When he or she comes, you remember nothing and when he or she goes away, only he or she is in your mind.
- His or her gait makes your heart go crazy.

23
What Gifts to Present to Your Friend

If you want to enter deep in a love relationship, then give your friend a lovely gift. The foundation of a relationship becomes strong if you present a sensible and meaningful gift to your friend. While presenting the gift, however, it is important to keep in mind the choice of your friend, occasion and time.

Flower – It is a symbol of beauty, attraction and tenderness. It will bring lovers close to each other. One can present a bouquet or a flower. You can present a basket bouquet or sometimes it can be presented by decorating the flowers in a pot.

Music – You can present your friend a CD, VCD or a cassette of romantic songs. Romantic songs will move his or her heart.

Books – You can present a romantic novel, a collection of stories, poems and arts, a book of jokes and other famous books. He or she will read them and get immersed in your love.

Greeting cards – Write your own poems, *ghazals* or lines of famous *shaiars* along with the lines given in the cards and send it across to him or her.

Cosmetics – This is a weakness of every young girl. The moment she receives a collection of cosmetic items, she will start doing make-up and look in the mirror in front of you. A boy will love to get an after-shave lotion from you.

Purse – A purse will enhance her personality. She will be excited to go shopping with you instantly. A boy can be presented a leather wallet.

Perfume – The perfume given by you will make her realise the depth of love and your presence. A boy would enjoy being gifted a subtle body spray.

Watch – The moving hands of the watch will make her realise that she has an absolute control over every moment of love. The same holds true for a boy.

Mobile – A mobile will end the distance between you and him or her. You can call up or send SMS messages whenever you like to him or her. You will feel closer, even if you may be far away.

Walkman – Gift a Walkman with your voice recorded in it. She or he can easily pass time whenever bored by listening to your voice.

Dress – You can present her a dress or a shirt to him that you want. She or he will be delighted after wearing the dress.

Diary – She or he can make a note of the times that you have spent with him or her and the times he or she spent without you. She or he will hold the diary against her or his chest as if it were you.

Pen – A pen will not be useful just for writing love letters and diary, it will also add to the collection of pens.

Photo album – She or he will feel the warmth of love when she or he will look at the photos of the beautiful moments spent togther.

Chocolate – After getting the chocolate, she or he will really be sweet. Chocolate is an all-time favourite gift.

Soft toys – She or he will talk about love by holding the toy against her or his chest.

Movies ticket – It will book two of you to experience the new feeling of love.

Jewellery – She or he will be shining by wearing these gifts. You will also say, 'Wow! If the jewellery is of gold, diamond or platinum, it's much better.' She will be in the seventh heaven after getting such gifts. A boy will enjoy getting cufflinks.

Spa treatment package – If your girlfriend is beauty conscious, then spa treatment package is the best gift to make her relax. She will like it very much. What else can be the gift as latest as this? For a boy too, it has become a welcome gift, provided they get the time.

Weekend tour - You feel like giving your friend a new gift even though you may have given several gifts, one after another. In order to present something new, an outing would be the best gift for him or her.

A word of caution

- Make sure you present the gift in a proper manner.
- Don't present transparent and bold outfts as gifts.
- If you want to give him or her a movie ticket, tell him or her one day in advance so that it does not spoil his or her schedule.
- Gift should not be heavy on your pocket.
- Don't borrow from your friend in order to buy a gift.
- Don't remind him or her of your gift repeatedly.
- Your gift to your friend should be according to the season. Don't give a winter gift in summer and summer gift in winter.
- Consider his or her hobbies, interests, likes and dislikes before presenting him or her a gift.

24
Flower Messages

Phool bhi kahate hain kahani,
agar na samajh payen toh
Yeh hai naadaani.

Even flowers tell a story,
if you don't understand,
then it is your ignorance.

If you want to express love in a different manner, you can send a gift of flowers. Flowers speak the language of the heart. There is a famous Persian poetry about the sweet language of rose published in A.D.1600 .

Charles II took poetry to Europe. In 1716, Lady Mary Wartley Montague took the flower language to England from Turkey. After that it reached France. Gradually, a 800-page book of flower messages got completed. After that the give-and-take of roses became so famous that today lovers from all over the world like to express love by giving roses. The flower expresses love somewhat in the following way:

- A red rose says, " I love you."
- A white rose says, "Our love is sacred."
- If red and white rose are given together, that means "unity."
- A red rose in full bloom says, "You are beautiful."
- A rose with two buds gives assurance of security.
- A closed bud of a white rose explains, "You are too little to fall in love."
- Yellow rose is somewhat suspicious and says, " I love you, but what is in your heart, I don't know."
- If there are leaves on the stalk, except thorns, then it means "There is nothing there. Neither there is fear nor there is any hope. In your beauty, I have somewhat lost all my sense."
- An orange rose says, "My love for you is infinite."
- The meaning of a bunch of roses with four leaves together – "Best of luck."
- A bud on a large branch arrogantly says, " I will love you. I am not afraid of anyone."
- A red rose and a single stalk means – "I am still in love with you."
- Jasmine rose – "I love you. Do you love me?" – one sided love.

- A red rose in full-bloom bouquet – "gratefulness, support and respect."
- A bud of rose with black colour - "Yes, I have loved you too."
- Blended rose – "I will always remember you."
- Two roses bound with a ribbon – "Already engaged."
- A fully bloomed rose in between two buds - "Secrecy."
- A crown of roses – "You got a prize. We are immensely pleased. Congratulations from my side."
- Wilted white rose – "Either you couldn't impress me or I don't love you."
- Deep burgundy rose – "You are unaware of your beauty."
- Brunette rose – "I will like you forever."
- Gardekisa – "You are lovely. Our love is secret."
- Aphelia – "Take care of yourself for the sake of me."
- A bunch of wilted flowers – "Your love is not acceptable to me."
- Orchids – "Awarded."
- Water lily – "Sanctity of heart."
- Henna – "Love and marriage relationship."
- Jasmine/ *juhi/ mogra* - "*Milan sarita.*"
- Jonquil – "Love me."

- Lilac – "First feeling of love."
- Acorn – "Life and immortality."
- Bitter sweet – "Truth."
- Bluebay – "Purity, tolerance."
- Cactus – "Tolerance."
- Cherry – "Good values and politeness."
- Cornflower – "Happiness."
- Narcissus – "You are the only one in the world."
- Dahlia – "Gaudiness."

25

Love Letters

Expressing one's love through love letters is a very old method. Today, writing love letters to a lover has reduced because of phones, mobiles, e-mails and SMS messages. But the importance of a love letter has not come to an end. Even today, lovers express their love through love letters.

A poet has said: "The lines have been erased like my hopes. But even today, the fragrance of your love letter has not gone."

Mit gaye meree ummeed ki tarha harf magar
aaj tak tere khaton se teri khushboo na gayee.

- Yes, you can erase the text of SMS, but the fragrance of a love letter will remain forever provided it is written in that style.
- Write your feelings openly in your letter, which will move the reader to the bottom of the heart.

- Always use polite and cultured language in love letters to show that you are a civilised person.
- Do not write a love letter on rejected, old and damaged paper. This shows the depth of your love.
- Don't write very long love letters. A short and sweet letter is enough to please him or her.
- Love letters written in a hurry, with dirty, crooked lines, scribbles and misspelt words, do not make a good impression.
- The language used in a love letter should express sweetness of love, intimacy, dedication and attraction.
- Don't write love letters threatening or flattering somebody.
- Don't write sexy, dirty, mean, pretended and untrue things.
- Do not write love letters when you are very exhausted or stressed. One tends to write wrong and inappropriate things at such times.
- Use figurative words in your love letters. You can use the first lines of some film song, poem or *ghazal*. This will make the portrayal of love more vivid.
- If you want to please your offended friend, you can take the help of a love letter.

26
Are You *Tingu?*

Don't be disappointed if you are shorter (Tingu) than your girlfriend. You can change your style of dressing and improve your height.

- Whenever you meet your girlfriend, don't wear the same coloured dress as her.
- When walking with your girlfriend or when you talk to her, keep your body straight.
- If you want to look thin and tall, wear oval, square or open T-shirts.
- Wear the dresses with thin and long lines. You will look taller in them.
- Wear high-heeled shoes or sandals when you go to see your girlfriend.
- Do not wear dresses having big patterns. You will look shorter in printed material.

- Do not gain weight. You will look shorter if you gain weight.
- Don't wear over-tight or over-loose dresses.

If the girl is too short, then she should

- Wear high heels always.
- Wear dresses with long lines or stripes on them.
- Always stand erect and sit upright when you are with your tall boyfriend.
- Wear plain pastel colours to look tall.
- Avoid putting on weight.

27

CU Some Time

If the warmth of love exists in two lovers, then they look for excuses to see each other every day. If there is a little lack in the warmth, the CU-Some-Other-Time situation comes into effect. In other words, business comes in between love. When you express your desire to meet, she or he makes an excuse by saying she or he does not have the time. It is but natural that you begin to think about so many other things. If there is CU-Some-Other-Time situation, then try to find out the reason behind it.

- ❤ Check to see if it is not infatuation which you thought to be love.
- ❤ See if the warmth of love has diminished between you.
- ❤ See if somebody else has come into the life of your girlfriend or boyfriend.
- ❤ Find out if you are showing too much love to him or her and which is putting him or her off.

- Perhaps you make your girlfriend or boyfriend stay late at night and make your friend receive scolding and nagging from the family.
- You may have some habit of yours which your friend does not like.
- It could be that you tease him or her when you meet and insist on having sex with you.
- It could be his or her job or profession that is not allowing him or her to find time for you.
- It could be that he or she spends most of the time on the internet with you and he or she does not have any time left to see you in person.
- During the initial days of a love-relationship there is a kind of excitement and eagerness to meet each other often. As time passes by, you know more and more about each other and as a result, you go back to catch up with your friends and relatives, because you had forgotten them for some time.
- Despite all these things, if there is CU-Some-Other-Time situation, do not take it for granted and let go, as it is a dangerous signal. Try to find out the cause immediately.

28

Don't Pay Highly for a Joke

When lovers speak to each other, they talk about different types of things. They crack jokes as well. Sometimes the joke is taken wrongly. A small joke can increase the distance between two lovers. Everybody does not have the ability to understand the meaning of the words spoken in jest. They misunderstand the meaning of these words. If your girlfriend or boyfriend takes jokes seriously, do not crack jokes with him or her. There are so many other topics to include in your conversation. Talk about those things that your girlfriend or boyfriend likes.

- Before saying anything, think carefully as to whether your friend will understand the words that you are about to utter.
- If she or he feels bad because of what you have said, then try to make it clear there and then. Don't let your friend go without getting the problem solved.

- If your girlfriend or boyfriend jokes, take it normally. If jokes are taken seriously, then there would be a crack in the relationship.
- Don't spoil your relationship by getting offended when your girlfriend or boyfriend jokes at you. Instead, laugh it off and avoid it.

29

In the Clutches of Your Friend

Has your world become limited to your girlfriend or boyfriend? If you have forgotten your family and friend circle because of your friend, then you have fallen into the hands of your boyfriend or girlfriend. So find out your own position by answering these questions.

- Do you spend most of your time with your girlfriend or boyfriend?
- Have you not been able to give even a little time to your family and friends?
- Do you cancel programmes regarding spending time with your family and friends at your girlfriend's or boyfriend's instructions?
- Do you think that it is your duty to fulfil every task of your girlfriend or boyfriend at any cost?
- In order to complete your girlfriend's or boyfriend's task, do you put off other tasks you are supposed to do?
- Does your friendship interfere in every affair of yours?

- Do you go running to your girlfriend or boyfriend whenever she or he calls you?
- Do you believe in whatever your girlfriend or boyfriend says?
- Would you choose your girlfriend or boyfriend if asked to make a choice between your friend and your family and other friends?
- Do you always sing praises about your girlfriend's beauty or your boyfriend's handsome looks?
- Do you blindly agree with your girlfriend or boyfriend without thinking over it?
- Would you agree if she or he says night to a day and day to a night? Or will you be willing to bring the moon to her or him?
- Do you do certain things on your girlfriend's or boyfriend's advice?

If the answer to most of the questions above is YES, then consider you are fully in the clutches of your girlfriend or boyfriend. Try to come out of it, otherwise, you know very well what the world will say to you.

30

Do not Forget

Pyar zindagi hai, pyar ke siwa kuchh bhi nahee.

(Love is life, there is nothing else besides love).

Have you gone so crazy in love that you have forgotten your meals, your job or business, your studies, your time-table and sleep? It is true, love is essential for life. That doesn't mean that you keep merely repeating it day and night and get drowned in the obsession.

- Don't forget the realities and priorities of life by becoming mad in love.
- Don't forget your family and friends for the sake of your girlfriend or boyfriend.
- Don't forget your future plans and your career in the obsession with love.
- Maintain your good relationships with people.
- Don't forget to take care of your body and health.
- Do not forget to pay respect to elders and treat with love those who are younger to you.

Under-cover relationship

- Many boys and girls draw a curtain on their romantic relationship by claiming to be a brother or sister. This is not a right thing to do.
- If you do love someone, then dare to make it public, because, if the truth of such a relationship comes out, both the families will be disappointed.
- If you're afraid of introducing yourself to your girlfriend's or boyfriend's family, then introduce yourself as her or his friend or classmate.
- Don't ask your girlfriend to tie a *rakhi*. This will degrade the dignity and splendour of the relationship.

31

Your Girlfriend/Boyfriend is not Your Private Property

Some youth have the habit of treating their girlfriend or boyfriend as their private property. They try to thrust their likes and dislikes, especially those people who are of dominating nature. They always try to control others. Later on they get left alone and become lonely.

To get rid of this problem, give up insistence or habit of saying that whatever you want must be done. Your girlfriend or boyfriend is, of course, yours but let her or him live one's own life. Don't try to exercise force and subdue her or him. Seeing that you behave like Hitler, she or he might be scared off.

- Do not thrust your likes or dislikes on your friend.
- Don't misunderstand when your girlfriend or boyfriend talks to your friend laughingly.
- Don't keep on singing your own tune. Listen to what your girlfriend or boyfriend has to say as well.

- Don't humiliate your girlfriend or boyfriend by calling her or him stupid, dull, dirty, etc.
- Don't fight if somebody accidentally bumps into your girlfriend or boyfriend or touches him or her.
- Don't interfere in his or her choice about food, dress and other things.
- Don't share his or her happiness only; share his or her sorrows as well.
- If you do not like anything about your girlfriend or boyfriend, do not say it in front of everybody. Convince him or her when he or she is alone, but don't shout at him or her or scold him or her. Make everything clear through patience and love.
- Don't pinch, touch, kiss and play with your friend's body parts. They are not your private property.
- Some girls and boys do not like people who hold hands, pull braids, pat cheeks, etc.
- Don't say in front of others that whatever you say, your girlfriend or boyfriend will willingly accept.
- Don't bet with your girlfriend or boyfriend in order to make her or him agree about anything.

32
Don't Doubt Your Friend

If one was to name the most dangerous man in the world, then most people would take the name of Hitler. But those people who doubt others are even more dangerous than Hitler. Even a tyrannical ruler will suffer a defeat in front of doubters.

In order to make your journey of love lovely, you should have equal respect, affection and intimate feelings for each other. Apart from this, there should be trust. If you doubt your girlfriend or boyfriend, your love cannot be pleasant. A love relationship is very delicate and it is based on the foundation of trust. If a split occurs in the relationship, then it is difficult to fill that split.

If there is frustration in your mind, then suspicion or doubt comes into existence. Psychologists call it a mental disease. In Shakespeare's Othello, *the hero Othello doubts his beloved Desdemona. He doubts even when her handkerchief falls accidentally. He thinks that his girlfriend drops her kerchief intentionally to indicate something to someone. This disease of doubting is also called 'Othello syndrome'.*

Another name for love is faith. If there is doubt instead, then a relationship does not last long. Such people get mentally frustrated, become very desperate and do not hesitate to commit the serious crimes.

Do you doubt?

- Do you keep a close watch on your friend?
- Do you inquire about him or her? Where does he or she go? Who does he or she meet? When does he or she reach home?
- Do you inquire about his or her friends and friend's circle?
- Do you check your girlfriend's or boyfriend's diary, purse, mobile as soon as you meet him or her?
- Do you call his or her office and ask about him or her?
- Do you go to his or her office and keep a watch?
- Do you enquire about him or her from the people at his or her office?
- Do you watch his/her colleagues in office?
- Do you fight with your girlfriend or boyfriend when he or she goes on a picnic with others?

If your answer to most questions is YES, then it is essential for you to change yourself. Otherwise, you will lose your girlfriend or boyfriend.

Why do you doubt?

You doubt if your girlfriend is beautiful; her personality is attractive; she uses lots of makeup; she is cheerful; she meets everyone without hesitation; she smiles at everyone while talking to them; she has the charm to attract others and she is at a good position.

Similarly, if your boyfriend is handsome, friendly and good-natured, do not doubt his intention. It may be his nature to be friendly with all.

Suggestions

- She is beautiful; she has a lot of admirers. But you have won the bet because you have already achieved her. This is your positive point. Nurture this feeling.
- If your girlfriend is too frank, then try to convince her.
- Speak openly when your girlfriend has any problem.
- Don't believe in hearsays or baseless stories.
- Keep yourself under control.
- He is good-looking, has girlfriends with whom he has a nodding acquaintance, is valiant and helps women of all ages. Accept him for what he is. After all he is close to you alone.
- Confide in your boyfriend and seek his advice if needed.
- Do not believe any stories you hear from others about your boyfriend without checking out first.

33

How to Please Your Offended Girlfriend / Boyfriend

Sulking and pleasing are part and parcel of every love relationship. A misunderstanding is developed between two lovers over a small matter. If this problem is not nipped in the bud, a breach occurs in the relationship.

When a boyfriend is offended. she pleases him easily by uttering three words "I am sorry". But it is difficult for a boy to say sorry because there is a man inside him. If one sees correctly, it is a small matter to soothe an offended person. According to a famous Arab storywriter, Kahlil Gibran, "It's a human weakness to make mistakes and to forgive is a human virtue. When they balance, there exists love."

- Then what's the point in taking anything so seriously?
- Don't take other's help to please your offended girlfriend or boyfriend?
- Ask the cause of her or his anger or annoyance.

- Give your explanation in front of him or her. Don't send it in the form of a message.
- Don't hesitate to say, "I am sorry", "I made a mistake", "Are you offended with me?" "And such a big punishment for such a small thing?". These words will move the heart of your girlfriend or boyfriend.
- You can please your offended girlfriend or boyfriend by sending a lovely message on your mobile.
- You can get rid of his or her misunderstanding by sending an e-mail or a greeting card.
- You can even present a chocolate bar, perfume, a make-up box and gently talk to your girlfriend and if your boyfriend is offended, persuade him to go out with you to watch a movie or on a picnic.

Also take care of these things

- Humiliating each other increases the distance between two lovers and offends both.
- If you demand to have sex, she may be offended or vice versa. This can even lead to a break-up of the relationship.
- Also, make sure that the girlfriend or boyfriend is not pretending to be offended or just playing with your feelings in order to fulfil his or her wishes.

34

Learn to Prasie Your Girlfriend / Boyfriend

According to psychologists, girls like to hear praise from their boyfriends. Same is the case with boys. A fashion designer, Sunanda Seth says that it is good to hear your boyfriend praise you, because it fills the mind with a renewed happiness, enthusiasm and excitement.

A film story-writer, Rama says, "I feel great when I hear my boyfriend praise me. It fills me with enthusiasm." So don't be stingy in praising your girlfriend or boyfriend.

The elegance of time: Pay attention to your girlfriend's or boyfriend's state of mind while praising him or her. Don't praise in a romantic way in front of his or her family members, office colleagues and friends.

Praise and boredom: It bores one to hear praise in the same manner again and again. For example, if you say, 'You are beautiful' again and again, then it becomes a very ordinary thing. Use new words, phrases and sentences to praise your girlfriend or your boyfriend.

Praise must not be dramatic and insincere: Yes, keep in mind that your praise should not sound dramatic and insincere. The words of praise should be from the bottom of your heart. Praising somebody as if you are making a speech would be considered dramatic and a pretence.

Don't praise by comparing: Don't compare your girlfriend or boyfriend with anybody. She or he will be hurt if you do so.

Natural state of your face: Take care of your facial expression while praising your girlfriend or boyfriend. You must take care of the body language so that it doesn't seem artificial.

False praise: Sometimes you need to make false praise.You must be extra careful in doing this, otherwise your move will backfire. Have you followed it?

On the phone or mobile: Times have changed. You can lavishly praise your girlfriend or boyfriend through SMS and Net chatting.

35
Handshake and Personality

The manner of handshake reveals the personality of a person. A body language expert, Tom Kel says, "You can read the personality of a person by looking at how he shakes hands." From the manner of handshake of your friend you can make out his or her personality and character.

- During the handshake, if your girlfriend or boyfriend keeps her or his one hand up and the other down, then consider that she or he wants to control you. She or he wants her or his friend to act on her or his instructions.
- If she or he covers your hand with her or his during a handshake, then understand that she or he likes you from the heart. She or he is willing to do anything for you.
- During the handshake, if your friend shakes hand lazily, then it indicates that she or he is not satisfied with you. She or he has taken for granted that her or his aspirations will not be fulfilled with you.
- The girl or boy who presses the hands forcefully during a handshake is considered arrogant, angry and disobedient.

- The girl or boy, who repeatedly shakes hands and strokes the hands is very sexy or selfish.
- If your girlfriend or boyfriend comes to your lap during a handshake, then that means she or he is afraid of something and she or he needs protection.
- The girl or boy who shakes hands warmly and kisses hands, is cheerful and clean-hearted.
- If a girl or boy shakes hands with two people, it means she or he has more than one boyfriends or girlfriends.
- The girl or boy with dirty, rough and filthy nails and who, you would not like to shake hands with can be a shirker, unhygienic and stubborn by nature.
- The girl or boy who just touches the fingers instead of the full hand can be very arrogant and selfish.

36

While Talking to Your Girlfriend / Boyfriend

Pay special attention to your voice and your choice of words while talking to your girlfriend or boyfriend.

- Don't shout at the top of your voice.
- Don't say anything without thinking.
- Do not speak by sprinkling spit.
- Don't tell lies about yourself and your family.
- Don't use obscene and foul words while talking to your girlfriend or boyfriend.
- Don't make fun of your girlfriend or boyfriend about anything.
- Don't burst into laughter while talking.
- Don't speak intimately in the first meeting. Don't be rude or too close to her or him.
- Don't just keep on talking about yourself. Let her or him speak too and listen attentively.

- Don't walk in the middle of the road when you are with your girlfriend or boyfriend.
- Do not claim what you say is right, best and appropriate.
- Do not utter anything bad by losing your temper with your girlfriend or boyfriend. Keep your cool and go ahead.
- Do not try to subdue your girlfriend or boyfriend while talking to her or him.
- Do not interrupt while your girlfriend or boyfriend is speaking. Joke with your friend lightly. Do not say anything that might hurt her or him.
- Don't get carried away by anything that your girlfriend or boyfriend says. Disagree diplomatically if you need to.
- Your subject of conversation should not be limited to sex, entertainment, films, sexy SMS, porn sites and MMS, etc.

37

Male or Female Colleague

In the course of day-to-day work, colleagues get to know each other well. It is not strange for two staff members to get close because of some official work and their association often develops into an emotional relationship. This continues to be alright till the management comes to know about it. When the fact is revealed, then a strange situation occurs. Sometimes, it gets to a stage where colleagues lose their job. So when your colleague is your girlfriend or boyfriend, it is essential to pay attention to certain things.

- If you have a colleague girlfriend or boyfriend, who is not always in a romantic mood, you should behave normally. Your attention should be on your work.
- Don't spend most of the time talking to your girlfriend or boyfriend or hanging around near her or his seat.
- Don't behave as lovers. Behave as normal colleagues.
- Don't remain stuck to the intercom or telephone.
- Don't hug or stick close to each other near the bathroom, corridor, steps and lift.

- Don't waste your time and others' by talking about yourself and your love.
- Don't go to movies with your girlfriend or boyfriend without informing. This would offend the management.
- Don't joke, tease, make fun or talk about your personal problems during office hours.
- Try to find a job for yourself and for your girlfriend or boyfriend in another company seriously.
- Do not forget the decorum of the office by drowning yourself in love. Discharge your duties well.
- If you make a girl your girlfriend or a boy your boyfriend, it is possible that some other staff who is trying to attract him or her toward himself or herself will be offended with you. In such situations, beware of the other staff members. They might provoke the management against you.
- Mind you, there are many cunning girlfriends or boyfriends who make their colleagues as their friends to achieve their selfish motives. After their work is done, they ditch the boyfriend or girlfriend just as a housefly is picked up from the milk and thrown.
- Do not quarrel with any staff member in order to impress your girlfriend or boyfriend.
- Do not forget to respect your seniors in order to make a good impression.

- Don't address your girlfriend or boyfriend as 'Darling,' 'Sweety,' 'My heart,' etc. in the office.
- Share your talks with other staff members as well. Be in tune with them.
- Do not find a pretext of going to your girlfriend's or boyfriend's seat and do not insist his or her hanging near you.
- If your girlfriend or boyfriend ignores you in office, instead of getting angry, try to understand her or him.
- If your girlfriend or boyfriend is the boss of your office, don't try to dominate other staff members.
- Do not doubt your girlfriend or boyfriend if she or he is friendly with other colleagues or nurture ill will against those staff members.
- If the management tells you to remain away from your girlfriend or boyfriend, then protest against it because they don't have any right to complain against the mutual relationship between two adults.

38

Quiet Girlfriend / Boyfriend

It is by nature that some people remain quiet. Those who keep quiet believe in the language of the eyes. They do not speak out what is in their heart but they say it all. If you want to make a girlfriend or boyfriend who happens to be quiet, then you should know a few things.

- When you propose to such a girl or boy, you will not understand her or him even if you get a reply.
- You fall a victim to depression if you fail to understand the feelings of such a girlfriend or boyfriend.
- There are some girls or boys who want boys or girls to hover around them, so they keep quiet. You must judge such types of girls or boys well.
- Know one thing more — you cannot share your thoughts, feelings, etc. fully with such types of girls or boys.
- To bring profoundness in your love, you must use words.
- Without words, you cannot make decisions about your future.

For your information

- Try to find out why your girlfriend or boyfriend is so quiet.
- It could be her or his nature since childhood or she or he may be trying to entice you on the pretext of it.
- It could be that somebody had attempted to rape her or in fact raped her. If she is victim of such a tragedy, try to console her.
- According to psychologists, it is a mental disease if a person keeps quiet. You can take your girlfriend or boyfriend to some psychiatrist.
- Try to know about her or his past. It could be that she or he has been thinking of some past incident because of which she or he is so quiet.
- Inquire about her or his family. It could be that because of her or his family circumstances that she or he is quiet. For instance, her or his mother has divorced her or his father; her or his father is a drunkard; her or his financial condition is bad; there has been a bereavement in the family, etc.
- Her ex-boyfriend or ex-girlfriend may have deceived him or her, because of whom, she or he is frustrated and sad.
- It could be that she or he wants her boyfriend or his girlfriend to hover around her or him and she or he is having fun, and she or he may be satisfied with what she or he is.

Take steps carefully

- First of all try to find out what she or he wants of you.
- If you don't get a satisfactory answer about this, it is better to say goodbye to such a person.
- It is better to change the path instead of being a victim of depression caused by the question – does she or he love me or not?

How to share your feelings with such a girlfriend or boyfriend

- When you meet your quiet girlfriend or boyfriend, always talk frankly about your thoughts and feelings.
- You can share your thoughts through SMS, MMS, phone or net chatting.
- Try to change the environment by taking her or him to another city. If you keep trying, her or his behaviour will certainly change.
- Always speak in a romantic mood. Watch romantic movies with her or him and discuss romantic topics with her or him.

Caution

- Do not insist on an answer to every question.

- Do not argue long about any topic with your girlfriend or boyfriend.
- Do not remain quiet with your quiet girlfriend or boyfriend, else there would be no one to break the ice.

39

Are You Stingy?

Girls are expert in making the pockets of boys empty, but there are some boys who are very clever in emptying the purses of girls or vice versa. Whether your girlfriend or boyfriend comes from a wealthy family or she or he is working, it is not a good idea to make her or him bear all expenses when you go out. Girls and boys get rid of such boys and girls. Judge whether you have the following habits:

- You don't spend on food and drinks when you take your girlfriend or boyfriend to a restaurant, hotel or other places.
- When you go to a hotel or a restaurant, you happen to be the first one to place an order. And you lag behind at the time of paying the bills.
- When you take your girlfriend or boyfriend out, you put the expenses on your girlfriend's or boyfriend's shoulders.
- You suggest going to the movies but you ask for advance money for the ticket from your girlfriend.

- When you take her or him on your bike or car, at the time of refuelling, you often say, 'I am sorry, I forgot my credit card.'
- When your girlfriend or boyfriend is with you, you use your mobile less and use your girlfriend's or boyfriend's mobile more to make calls.
- You become very happy when your girlfriend or boyfriend gives you a gift. You sing praises of him or her, and you don't even think of presenting a gift yourself because you have to spend money on it.
- You pretend to look like a wretched or miserable creature so that he or she doesn't demand anything for which you have to pay.

Points to remember

- A girl or boy likes you, but she or he does not say anything even though you behave like a miser. This does not mean that you take advantage of her or his simplicity.
- No matter how rich your girlfriend or boyfriend is, her or his parents, brothers and sisters must be asking her or him to give an account of the expenses. She or he might even have to tell lies due the expenses incurred on you.
- If your girlfriend or boyfriend is an employee, then many people may be dependent on her or him. If she or he spends money on you, she or he might have to cut down on other expenses.

- Mind you, if you think your girlfriend or boyfriend is your ATM card, she or he can also think you are her or his credit card and cash in on you.
- You are a man, behave like a man. Don't have fun with your girlfriend's money. Have you got it or not ? At times this applies to girls too.

40

Oedipus Love

There were times when a boy used to make a girl his friend of his own age. Now the times have changed. Now boys want to make girlfriends older than themselves. Sachin Tendulkar's wife Anjali is five years older than him. Azharuddin's wife Sangeeta is many years older than Azhar. If your girlfriend is older than you, there shouldn't be any inferiority complex.

In today's world, it is a common thing to do such a thing. Falling in love with an older girl is called an Oedipus love.

- If you are into an Oedipus love, don't nurture any fear in your heart — what will people say? Instead, try to nurture the thought that - people are people, they will talk anyway.
- Be cheerful whenever you are with your girlfriend or boyfriend. She or he will also be happy and cheerful.
- Don't feel bad about introducing your girlfriend to others. Introduce her with pride saying, "This is my girlfriend." This applies to boyfriends too.

- Don't make your girlfriend wear dresses meant for teenagers in an attempt to make her look younger. It would seem odd.
- Be like a mature person in front of your girlfriend. Don't make her feel that you're younger than her.
- Don't hide your Oedipus love. By doing so, you will not be doing justice to your love. It is your love; hiding it would be inappropriate.

41

When a Girl or Boy is after You

Sometimes the situation gets really tough when a girl or boy is after you to make you her boyfriend or girlfriend and you don't like that person. It is difficult to get rid of such a girl or boy. If you are trapped in such a situation, then you don't need to panic, or lose your cool, or compromise and become a scapegoat. You can get rid of this trouble by using a little bit of wisdom.

- If you are hounded by any girl or boy, don't lose your cool. Try to solve the problem.
- First of all, find out why she or he is attracted to you. Find out the reason and try to change your behaviour.
- It could be that she or he is under a false impression that you love her or him. If that is so, try to remove her or his mistaken belief.
- If the girl or boy is of tender age, tell her or him about the high and low, good and bad of social life. Tell her or him to pay attention to studies, rather than fall in love blindly.

- In order to get rid of the girl or boy chasing you, send a message telling her or him that you don't like her or him and you are not interested in her or him, and that you are already in love with someone else.
- You can talk to her or his family and your family about it.
- Don't delay in getting rid of the girl or the boy. As the days pass by, love for you will keep on increasing.
- Try to avoid her or him somehow if she or he wants to come to you.
- Don't try to talk to her or him or meet her or him. If possible don't respond properly to what she or he says.
- Don't promise her or him anything even by mistake. Also, don't look down on her or him or criticise her or him in front of others.
- Discourage her or him straight away if she or he tries to get closer to you.

42

Girlfriend's / Boyfriend's Sister / Brother

Many boys consider their girlfriend's sister as their sister-in-law, which is not appropriate. The relationship between you and your girlfriend's sister is very delicate. Even a small mistake will create a split between you and your girlfriend. Your attitude towards your girlfriend's sister should be very polite and courteous. The same holds true for girls. Too much familiarity with the boyfriend's brother can breed contempt.

- Do not behave with your girlfriend's sister as your sister-in-law. Similarly a girl should not show too much proximity to her boyfriend's brothers.
- Don't talk to your girlfriend's sister too intimately. Don't try to be too close to her. Same holds true for girls also.
- Don't assent to whatever your girlfriend's sister asks for. It may create a misunderstanding.
- Do not go to movies or shopping with your girlfriend's sister separately. Similarly do not go out alone with your boyfriend's brother.

- Don't present any expensive gifts to your girlfriend's or boyfriend's brother or sister.
- It is not advisable to send her or him a greeting card or wish her or him on special days.
- Don't throw a party even if it is your girlfriend's sister's birthday or your boyfriend's brother's birthday.
- Don't praise your girlfriend's sister in front of your girlfriend or your boyfriend's brother in front of him.
- Don't buy a gift for your girlfriend's sister or for your boyfriend's brother along with other gifts for your girlfriend or boyfriend.

43

Friend of Your Girlfriend / Boyfriend

Misunderstandings often happen because of a girlfriend's or boyfriend's friend. As a result, a split occurs between the two lovers and the relationship between them may come to an end. If your girlfriend's or boyfriend's friend is smart and goodlooking, then the matter will be even more serious.

- You must be cautious if your girlfriend's or boyfriend's friend is being attracted to you.
- If your girlfriend's or boyfriend's friend is drawn towards you, then check to see if you are at all trying to attract her or him.
- If she or he is attracted to you because of your personality, give full information about it to your girlfriend or boyfriend.
- Don't reject directly if your girlfriend's or boyfriend's friend proposes to you. Try to avoid her or him indirectly.
- Don't discuss with your girlfriend's or boyfriend's friend your girlfriend's or boyfriend's problem. In doing so, she or her will try to get close to you.

- Don't make any programmes to meet, to go shopping, to go on a picnic or to any other event with your girlfriend's or boyfriend's friend. This might create a misunderstanding between you and your girlfriend or boyfriend.
- If your girlfriend's or boyfriend's friend has invited you to some programme, then take your girlfriend or boyfriend along with you.

44

Why Somebody Else's Girlfriend / Boyfriend Seems Nice?

Often, others' girlfriends seem nice to most youngsters, even though they may have smart and beautiful girlfriends. In such situations, boys attract to others' girlfriends even though they have their own girlfriend. Why do boys behave like this? Dr Arun Kumar Gupta of Ram Manohar Lohia Hospital, New Delhi has the answer to the question. Every youngster has a dream about his girlfriend. His girlfriend would be like this, or she would be like that. If he doesn't find these qualities in his girlfriend, he begins to look at others' girlfriends. Beauty attracts everybody. Boys try to attract any girl who is more beautiful than their girlfriend. The same is true for your boyfriend's friends. You seem attracted to them if they are better in any way than your boyfriend.

- Some boys and girls have the habit of behaving abnormally when they see a girl or a boy. Sometimes they even forget that they have a girlfriend or boyfriend.
- When a boy or girl gets bored with a girlfriend or boyfriend, he or she gets drawn towards others' girlfriend or boyfriend.

- Until somebody gets what he or she wants, he or she is interested in that thing. Once he or she gets that thing, the charm vanishes. After achieving a girlfriend or boyfriend, boys and girls do not have so much of attachment to their girlfriend or boyfriend as they did before. So they start getting attracted to others' girlfriend or boyfriend.
- If the girlfriend or boyfriend is lavish in expenditure, arrogant and insults others, then these are minus points that drive a boy or girl away from their girlfriend or boyfriend.
- Their attention is more towards others' girlfriend or boyfriend instead of their own.
- Dr Gupta says, "Stay away from attractions. You must be committed to one person."
- If your love is true, then you should not pay attention to others' girlfriends or boyfriends.
- If you notice any weakness in your girlfriend or boyfriend, you should try to correct it.

45

Your Girlfriend/Boyfriend can be Your Dreaded Enemy

Times have changed. Now the girl or boy you love more than your life could turn out to be your killer.

There have been so many such cases in the country in which a girl killed a boy or boy killed a girl pretending to be her or his boyfriend or girlfriend. Cunning and crafty girls and boys easily trap naive boys and girls in their web of false love. The boys and girls are easily taken in by subtle behaviour and the boys end up losing their lives.

Points to remember

- Be careful if your girlfriend or boyfriend gives more importance to your wealth than you.
- Don't make someone your girlfriend or boyfriend who goes to dance bars and is very cunning and crafty.
- Be careful of your girlfriend or boyfriend who thinks you are a lottery ticket.

- Beware, if your girlfriend or boyfriend always asks about your income and wants to see your bank passbook, payslip and your property document.
- Be careful if your girlfriend or boyfriend pretends to be in love with you, extracts money by smooth talk and even tempts you to go to bed with her or him, and blackmails you.
- Find out from your girlfriend's or boyfriend's background if her or his father, brothers, or any relative is a criminal. It could be that she or he has some purpose to come in contact with you.
- When a boyfriend begins to have an affair with another girl, his girlfriend gets deeply hurt. As a result, out of anger she kills her boyfriend.
- If you come from a rich family, take extra care to choose your girlfriend or boyfriend. Even mafia gangsters make use of beautiful girls or young boys to trap the wealthy and kidnap them to extract money from their families.

46
Publicity of Love

Boys keep advertising their love, whereas girls don't want any publicity of love. Girls don't want their love to be disgraced. On the other hand, boys make a fuss about their love.

Why do they do like this?

- That there is someone who dies for them.
- That they have certain qualities because of which boys or girls are after them.
- That they have done a big job by attracting a beautiful girl or a handsome boy.
- They feel good about having the publicity given to their love.

Points to remember

- As far as possible don't publicise your love.
- A girl or even a boy can get into trouble with her or his friends and relatives because of publicity.

- Boys make up stories when they see their friend's girlfriend as if she is a prostitute.
- Some boys tease their friend's girlfriend saying 'Bhabhi' or something else.
- They crack sexy jokes as if she is your sister-in-law.
- Don't speak loudly, laugh loudly or scream in public places.
- Girls believe in hiding and the boys believe in showing their love.
- Love with your eyes. Don't utter the word in public places.
- Try to listen to her silent request in her eyes. She does not want love to be publicised.
- If you are a true lover, speak softly, so that no one hears you.

47

Lying Girlfriend / Boyfriend

Many girls and boys have the habit of telling lies. They tell lies to other friends. But true lovers do not tell lies to each other.

Telling lies is a mental disease. According to psychologist Dr A.D. Nayyar from Hindu Rao Hospital, a person suffering from this disease makes an imaginary picture of some person. He or she becomes used to this habit. According to psychologists, telling lies is a mental disease called mythomania.

You recognise a person from the body language. He or she has to face a lot of problems because of telling lies. Telling lies creates a lot of problems so we must be aware of such girls and boys.

- If you come to know that the girlfriend or boyfriend tells lies, then try to convince her or him that it is not a good idea. If she or he doesn't mend her or his ways then it would be better if she or he is kept quiet.

- Judge your girlfriend's or boyfriend's behaviour and gestures in order to find if she or he tells lies.
- Your girlfriend or boyfriend thinks of himself or herself as a hi-fi person and exaggerates everything.

Don't rush to get rid of your lying girlfriend or boyfriend.

48

When Somebody Cheats on You in Love

It is not surprising that in times of MTV culture, boys get deceived by their girlfriends and vice versa. It hurts you to find out that the person who you dearly loved has deceived you.

- Before falling in love, try to collect full information on your girlfriend or boyfriend.
- Many girls trap boys or boys trap girls in their net and into a relationship. They even secretly photograph their romantic activities and blackmail them later.
- If your girlfriend or boyfriend deceives you, then try to forget her or him. Be thankful that it was good that you came to know of it before it was too late. Otherwise, she or he would have continued to deceiving you all your life.

49
Love and Unfaithfulness

"Hum bewafa hargiz na the,
magar hum wafa kar na sake."

Unfaithfulness is such a word that lovers are scared to think of it. Getting in a frenzy due to unfaithfulness, several lovers become wild and kill their girlfriends. They even resort to blackmailing them, so much so that they even commit suicide.

First of all, for your information, love and unfaithfulness are two faces of the same coin, so don't take it so seriously.

If your love is true, then you should have the courage to bear unfaithfulness.

If your girlfriend or boyfriend is unfaithful or deceives you, then consider that he or she must have had some valid reason behind it.

Because of family pressure, sometimes your girlfriend or boyfriend may begin to distance herself or himself, so try to understand her or his problem.

Your girlfriend or boyfriend will dump you if you neglect your future plan, career or ambition.

Your girlfriend or boyfriend will detach herself or himself from you if your ideas and behaviour do not match.

If you seduce your girlfriend or boyfriend to have physical relationship with you or put pressure on her or him to do something wrong, she or he might like to stay away from you.

Watch out!

Many boys or girls begin to go around with other girls or boys in order to get close to their girlfriends or boyfriends. Instead of teasing or making her or him jealous by being friendly with others, try to take notice of the following:

- Remember, you cannot force somebody to love you and also you cannot get somebody's love by force.
- In order to tease your girlfriend or boyfriend or make him or her jealous, do not make friends with other girls or boys. This will hurt her or him very much.
- Try to find out why your girlfriend or boyfriend has gone far from you. After knowing the reason, try to find a solution.

50
Unfaithful Lover

Gone are the days when a girlfriend or boyfriend used to be devoted to her boyfriend or girlfriend. For some women and men even the concept of love has changed. It has become a fashion to make boyfriends and girlfriends. They change their friends as soon they see a car instead of a bike, and a huge bank balance instead of a car. It is better to die than to slog for such a girlfriend or a boyfriend. You have to be practical about such things.

- When you are certain that your girlfriend or boyfriend is beginning to have an affair with somebody else, talk to her or him about it frankly.
- Do not go out of control when see your girlfriend or boyfriend with somebody else. First of all, try to find out who he or she is and what is their relationship.
- If your girlfriend or boyfriend says he is her or his cousin, then don't say anything. If she or he meets the cousin very often, then try to find out the truth of the relationship.

- If your girlfriend or boyfriend says she or he is just her friend, don't say anything to her or him in front of her or him. After he or she goes away, you tell him or her outright that you don't approve of meeting somebody else like this. You will be able to see her or his reaction to this.
- Even after your objections, she or he keeps meeting that boy or girl, take it for granted that you are going to be sidelined.
- When you feel that your love relationship is going to break, then try to find a solution to the problem with your girlfriend or boyfriend. For that you can even include her or his new friend.
- Make your friend realise that you are more worthy than the other guy or girl.
- See if your girlfriend or boyfriend has the habit of flirting with others. If she or he always behaves flirtatiously, then it will be difficult for you to change her or him. It would be better you changed your path.
- It is not right to scold, scream or howl at your girlfriend or boyfriend.
- Don't scold her or his new friend in front of your girlfriend or boyfriend. It would sound uncouth and people will laugh at you.

- Tell her or his new boyfriend or girlfriend about your relationship in detail, so that he or she would know that the girl or boy who he or she is in love with was somebody's before.
- It is not appropriate to spend your life brooding over your unfaithful girlfriend or boyfriend.You should go ahead by facing the realities with courage.
- Don't think of committing suicide for your unfaithful girlfriend or boyfriend and forget your parents and siblings. In doing so, your family will be in pain and they will not bear the disgrace.

51

When You are Unsuccessful in Love

Alok was an unsuccessful lover. The girl he was in love with, didn't love him. Then what? He resorted to sleeping pills as he became unsuccessful in love and considered life to be disappointment and misery.

Another incident is of Meera who lands up in hospital in a serious condition. Despite all the efforts, the doctors cannot save her. She had committed suicide by taking poison. From the letter written by her, found in her room, it could be inferred that Meera was in love with a boy named Apurva. Apurva got married to somebody else. Meera couldn't live without Apurva, so she committed suicide.

The third incident is of Rinku's murder at Ulhasnagar in Maharashtra. The murderer Haresh Patel liked Rinku Patil. He used to love her. But Rinku didn't want to get into any relationship with him. Then what? Unsuccessful as he was in love, Haresh Patel entered the examination hall during an exam and set fire on Rinku.

In the fourth incident, Rakesh loved Sonali. Here Sonali had been avoiding Rakesh for some days, because she was going to be married soon. Rakesh could not tolerate Sonali avoiding him like that and that she was going to be married to somebody else. As soon as he got an opportunity along with his friends, he raped Sonali. Sonali died as she could not bear the humiliation.

The fifth incident is about a factory worker in Goregaon, named Amarjit, who wanted to achieve his beloved's love but something was preventing him. He made up his mind to get his beloved by any means. In an attempt to do so, he killed eight innocent people along with the owner. Today, he is spending his life behind bars.

We see such incidents every day. The gist of the above incidents is that you end up taking wrong decisions if you are unsuccessful in love. It is a natural phenomenon that sexual attraction draws a boy and a girl close to each other. If love becomes unsuccessful, then it gives rise to wrong and negative activities (murder, suicide, alcoholism, rape, etc.) and that brings disgrace upon oneself and the society. Let's analyse the first incident. The love between Alok and his girlfriend was one-sided as the girl didn't love him. So there is no question of being successful or unsuccessful. Although Alok was a good person, he was frustrated because of the thoughts that came into his mind — Am I so bad that nobody loves me? Can't I love? Don't I have a good personality? As he was frustrated with all these things, he took to drinking alcohol. But, instead of blaming himself, he blames his so-called girlfriend. If Alok had wanted, he could have become her friend, mate or companion.

Was it essential for Alok to get her as his girlfriend?

In the second incident, Meera considered her boyfriend unfaithful. If your boyfriend marries another person, why call him unfaithful? Was it necessary to marry only her boyfriend? Meera didn't think of the boyfriend who she loved so much, before committing suicide. If she had thought properly, she would not have committed suicide. He must have had some obligation. Would it have been right to destroy the hopes of his parents? Should he have eloped with Meera and got married somewhere?

The last incidents are painful. Rinku Patil's murderer, Haresh Patel never loved Rinku at all. That's why he did not think before killing his girlfriend. Behind Rinku's murder the only intention was: "If you cannot be mine, you cannot be anybody else's."

Haresh did not try to find out the cause of the death of the love relationship. If Haresh had known, he would have earned Rinku's love by mending his ways. What did Haresh get after killing her? Similarly Amarjit did not get love either, even after killing eight people. He is behind bars today and suffering his punishment.

If you take a look at history, you can find several unsuccessful lovers as examples. Although they suffered frustrations in their personal lives, they became famous by their achievements.

The great leader, Napoleon Bonaparte loved his beloved

Josephine wholeheartedly, but he couldn't win her love. A German poet, Gert, loved a beautiful girl Charlet, but Gert's love was unsuccessful in making any deep impression on Charlet. As Charlet didn't pay any attention to his love, he disappeared and slipped away quietly without informing Charlet.

Nobel Prize winner, Rabindranath Tagore loved a 17-year old girl Anna, but he could not achieve her love. He named his love Nalini. He wrote a play by the same name, which became very popular. He immortalised his love by doing so.

- The unsuccessful should try to find out the cause of being rejected.
- If your love is one sided, don't be serious. Try to propose to another person similar in looks, behaviour and stature.
- Don't just go after good looks, because several other guys or girls will also be dying for the girl or boy.
- Before proposing to any girl or boy, consider your complexion, behaviour, status and personality so that your request will not go waste.
- If you are unsuccessful in love, you should muster enough courage and face the realities.
- Don't thrust yourself in the world of sorrow and loneliness considering that it is your fate to be unsuccessful in love.
- If the injury is new, it hurts. But if you apply medicine, it heals fast.

- Sometimes the injury leaves its mark and sometimes nothing remains.
- Don't think about taking revenge if you are unsuccessful in love. Don't try to destroy her or him. If you do so, it would be a war, not love.
- Just as there is a new day after every night, it could be that you are going to get a far better lover than the present one.

52

When You have a Break-up with Your Girlfriend / Boyfriend

After breaking up with your girlfriend or boyfriend, there is immense grief in your heart. Nothing comes to your mind as the one with whom you dreamt of living your life together, has left you. You get so angry that you feel like setting fire to the entire world. You get so confused that life seems to have come to a halt. Life seems to be a burden. Every person cannot tolerate the trauma of a heart-break. Those who have a weak heart, they go crazy. Many boys and girls even go to the extent of committing suicide.

It needs courage to go ahead after a break-up. Instead of shedding tears all day long, cursing your destiny and God, one should take life under control. You must understand that it is not a film story, where one has to change roles — sometimes you become a mad person or sometimes you need to commit suicide, depending upon the nature of the script. Accept break-up as a normal thing in real life. Try to bring your life on track again. Let bygones be bygones. Accept the present realities of life.

Causes of break-up

- Lukewarm in love life.
- Advent of artificiality in love.
- Slack in income, increase in aspirations.
- Lack of mutual understanding.
- Entrance of 'she/he' in between we/us and you.

Essential tips

- Don't waste time shedding tears day and night.
- Console yourself by saying that if she or he can stay without me, why cannot I?
- Just because somebody goes away from your life, the world does not come to an end.
- Let bygones be bygones. Whatever has happened, it is over and done with.
- Relieve your heart by telling your tale to any intimate friend of yours.
- Don't try to bring back your girlfriend or boyfriend who has left.
- Don't be miserable and woebegone and go showing your pain to others.
- Don't discuss your broken-up love life with your family, friends and relatives. And also, don't let them discuss it.

- Don't be careless about your health. Otherwise, you will fall into a deep pit of depression and frustration.
- Don't take drugs or resort to alcoholism to forget your girlfriend or boyfriend.
- Get rid of the memories of your ex-girlfriend or former boyfriend by destroying her or his love letters, gifts and photos.
- Don't plan to do any harm or take revenge on your girlfriend or boyfriend.
- Don't get into the rut of astrology, palmistry and black magic.
- Take a break and go on a tour, away from your city.
- Begin searching for a new girlfriend or boyfriend saying that if one goes away, there is another in the line.
- You will get lots of other opportunities to win love. You just have to step ahead once again. There must be somebody or other waiting for you.

53

Trapping Girl/Boy is not Ethical

Some boys and even girls cast such an impression on girls or boys that they get trapped in their snares. After having enough fun with a girl or boy, they look for another girl or boy. Trapping girls or boys and playing with their lives is not at all a good idea. It should not be done.

- Adopt a positive attitude towards the girl or boy you wish to make your girlfriend or boyfriend.
- Don't play with the emotions and body of the girl or boy after they fall in love with you.
- If seeing any girl or boy turns you on, then you only have the body of the girl or boy.
- To trifle with the emotions of others can be dangerous. It can be fatal.
- Those who are professional deceivers, they try to trap girls and boys from rich and affluent families. They have fun with them by extracting money from them.

54

Love is not a Bed of Roses

Love is life. Smiling and crying are part and parcel of life. Love makes one laugh and also makes one cry. If you love somebody, don't take it for granted that you will get love lifelong. You may get pain and suffering too. A renowned philosopher, Belle says the sweetest and bitterest pain in life is love.

After achieving love, lovers take the flight to the land of fantasy. When love ceases to give company, the plane of fantasy crashes all of a sudden with a thud. Some boys and girls cannot tolerate the pain of separation from love. They go crazy and wander around, heart-broken. They even think of committing suicide. Some become Shirin or Farhad and turn to alcoholism.

- If your love is true, then keep in mind that love can make you laugh as well as cry.
- "Oh, I will die if I don't marry you. I will remain a bachelor all my life." Saying such childish things are not appropriate.

- Don't think of committing suicide if your girlfriend or boyfriend is offended. Only those who are weak think of doing so.
- If your girlfriend or boyfriend gets married to somebody else, don't take it badly. Console yourself by saying that she or he must have had some problem.
- Sacrifice yourself in love and be an example for others.
- It is not necessary that your girlfriend or boyfriend will surely be yours. It is possible that she or he will change according to the times.
- While walking the path of love, don't just think about pizzas and burgers. Have a taste of gram and *lai-chana* as well sometimes.

55
Magic and Witchcraft for Love

Since time immemorial, magic and witchcraft have been very common among people to attract others of the opposite sex. Even today, in the scientific era, magic, hypnotism, etc. are being practiced to win over love. Several tribal castes in India adopt methods to win the love of the opposite sex.

In Madhya Pradesh, a tribesman somehow obtains a dress of the girl whose love he wants to win. He burns the dress to ashes. Out of mud of a hill, he makes a statue. After putting vermillion, lemon juice, etc. on it, he keeps the statue in the middle of the jungle. It is believed that by doing so, the girl will go crazy and come running to the boy.

A youth of a nomadic tribe makes a crooked and rough image of a girl on whom he wants to cast a magical spell with his blood or vermillion on birch-tree leaf. The leaf is packed in a copper case. And then the boy wears it around his arm as a talisman. It is believed that the girl gets bewitched and falls under the boy's spell.

In Korku tribe, a boy makes a wish to win the love of a girl he desires at any temple and makes a promise by saying, "Get me this girl. I will offer a sacrifice of a black hen if my wish is fulfilled."

Boys from Kanjar tribe somehow get hold of three strands of hair of the girl whose love they want to achieve. After keeping the strands of hair overnight with them, they put them in a hole of a tree. They believe that as the tree grows, the strands of hair will also grow and love will multiply. After 21 days, the girl would become crazy about the boy and she would come running to him.

Enchanted by their beauty, boys taking to magic and witchcraft to subdue girls is very common. In a tribal caste, even a girl resorts to witchcraft when attracted by a boy. The girl makes a strange shape on a banana leaf. While making the drawing, she spells out the name, village and the identity of the boy and says that she loves him. "May he become crazy for my love. May I get him. We will worship you together on the bank of a river." She buries the leaf on the bank of the river. It is believed that after 40 days, she will win her love.

A youth of Haiti Island belonging to a tribal group writes the name of the person he wants to enchant on a leaf of a special tree and lets it float on the ocean for 40 days. He does not eat anything during this period.

The people believe that in doing so, the boy's wish will be fulfilled. The practice of magic and witchcraft is also common abroad. A girl in Hungary takes a little soil out of a grave and puts it in a pouch and places the pouch under her pillow. It is believed that by doing so, the boy will lose his peace of mind and fall in lovewith the girl.

In Europe, a heart-shaped root is a bestseller. A boy buys it and buries it in front of the girl's house. It is believed that within 21days, the girl falls in love with the boy. A special type of cake is sold in Western countries. The cake-seller says that if the cake is fed to a girl of one's choice, she begins to long for him.

56

Valentine's Day

Valentine's Day is that day when the seed of love germinates and sprouts. It is a special day for those who love truly. True love expects friendship, dedication and sacrifice. This special day for true lovers began to be celebrated as Valentine's Day 800 years ago in Rome. This day, which is a day for expressing one's love, was the day of sacrifice for love of St. Valentine.

During the reign of Claudius II, a Roman king, the soldiers were prohibited from falling in love and getting married. The king considered love to be absurd and he hated those people who loved. Pope Giletius protested against this law. He secretly got a soldier married. When King Claudius got to know about it, he had Giletius arrested and put in jail. And he gave the order to hang him. While Giletius was in jail, he married the blind daughter of the jailer. It is said that because of the power of love, the blind girl got back her sight. But Giletius's death sentence remained valid. When he was being taken to the death-bed on 14 February 269 A.D., he wrote the last love letter to his beloved. At the bottom of the letter he wrote, "From your Valentine."

The 14th of February is celebrated as the day of romance. Nobody knows for sure who found out this truth. But those who are in love, they find out some way or other to celebrate, whether it is on the pretext of history or to mark the start of the romantic spring season.

57

I Love U 2

The meaning of 'I-Love-U-2' sounds obvious. Some boys keep two girlfriends instead of one. They get pleasure in doing so. According to a psychologist, Dr Rocklin Way, the definition of love is changing fast. Earlier a lover was willing even to die for the sake of his beloved. Now they keep two girlfriends. Even girls are not behind in this matter. Even after knowing that the boy has an affair with another girl, she proposes to him.

Why do they do like this?

- What good have you done if you love only one girl or one boy? Have fun with several girls.
- Boys think it is a new world. When girls cannot stick to one boy, then why can't boys have fun with at least two girls?
- Boys think, "If it is valid in films like '*Gharwali Baharwali*,' why can't we fall in love with two girlfriends?"

- Boys and girls think if Draupadi had five husbands, why can't they have two girlfriends or boyfriends?
- Girls think that there is not one but two boys who are dying for me. To be in love with only one is outdated. It belongs to Adam's era.
- It is difficult to put your legs in two boats. It needs great courage to do so. Everyone cannot do this. But I will show it.

Cut two out

- There is no space between you and I. So don't fall in love with two instead of one.
- I-love-U-2 situation can be very dangerous sometimes. It can even take someone's life.

58

Girlfriend / Boyfriend and Your Friend

No matter how close you are to your friend, keep several things in mind when you introduce your girlfriend or boyfriend to him or her. First of all, whenever you introduce your girlfriend or boyfriend to your friend, don't leave or him her alone with him or her because when two opposite sexes meet each other, there is a certain chemical reaction that attracts them. This attraction can put you in trouble.

- Don't compliment your friend's capabilities.
- Don't leave your girlfriend or boyfriend with your friend alone and go somewhere else.
- If you are playing a game, be your girlfriend or boyfriend yourself.
- Don't make your friend of her or his partner.
- When you eat at a restaurant, both of you can eat from the same plate. Ask for a separate plate for your friend.

- When you go to watch a movie, sit in between your girlfriend or boyfriend and your friend.
- When there is an argument about anything, support your girlfriend or boyfriend instead of your friend.
- Don't let it happen that your friend's and your girlfriend's or boyfriend's views, qualities and personality are similar and yours are different from them.
- Don't praise your friend in front of your girlfriend or boyfriend, no matter how close he or she is to you.

59

Never Interfere in Your Friend's Family Matters

Avoid getting into the domestic affairs or family matters of your girlfriend or boyfriend and interfere in them. It could be that your girlfriend or boyfriend will not like your interference in her or his personal problems. Because of such behaviour of yours, she or he might distance herself or himself from you.

- Limit your interference in the family affairs of your friend to a certain extent.
- Advise your girlfriend or boyfriend when she or he asks for your advice. Whenever you advise her or him, be appropriate and reasonable.
- Let your girlfriend or boyfriend live her or his own life.
- If your girlfriend or boyfriend is in trouble, try to do your best to help.
- Encourage your girlfriend or boyfriend to face the difficulties.

60

If Your Friend is too Materialistic

There were times when girls used to be impressed by education and personality of boys. But today, they ask about their bank balance. In practical life, a girlfriend has the right to know about her boyfriend's income or bank balance. But if the girl is too concerned about his balance sheet, then she does not love him for the sake of love, but for the sake of money. Today with many girls working, it is possible for a boy to love her for her money.

- The girl or boy who asks about your bank balance does not love you.
- To know about the financial condition of her boyfriend or girlfriend, he or she takes him or her to expensive restaurants.
- She or he asks for expensive gifts.
- She or he tries to lure her boyfriend or girlfriend excessively and praises him or her.
- She or he borrows money from the boyfriend or girlfriend, pretending to be in a miserable condition.

- Her or his eyes are always on your wallet or your ATM card.

Your girlfriend or boyfriend will doubt you when you behave in these ways

- When her boyfriend or his girlfriend is having a hard time financially, she keeps a watch on her boyfriend and he on his girlfriend.
- He or she asks his girlfriend or boyfriend to pay the bill after eating at a restaurant.
- He or she uses his girlfriend's or boyfriend's credit card for petrol refuelling.
- Before buying any gift for his girlfriend or her boyfriend, he or she says, 'Not now, but will buy later.'
- If you have any such habit, watch out. Your girlfriend or boyfriend might try to find out about your financial status at such times. So mend your ways.

61

Restaurant Manners

When you go to a restaurant, you should know the etiquettes. If you don't behave properly at a restaurant, the fun of eating will be spoiled and you will be a subject of ridicule.

- Don't phone and ask your girlfriend or boyfriend to reach a particular restaurant and that you will catch up there.
- If you want to go to a restaurant, go together with your girlfriend or boyfriend.
- It is better to book a table before going to a restaurant.
- When you reach a restaurant, don't rush for the empty table. Wait for the waiter to show you the table.
- If you don't like the table, ask the waiter politely to give another table.
- Don't place an order for the food of your choice before reaching a restaurant. Ask what your girlfriend's or boyfriend's choice is.

- Don't just order food of your choice only. Insist that your girlfriend or boyfriend orders the food of her or his choice.
- Confirm with your girlfriend or boyfriend before ordering the food.
- Don't speak loudly and argue with your friend at a restaurant.
- To call a waiter, say, 'Excuse me' politely or lift your hand gently.
- If anything falls, call the waiter instead of picking it up yourself.
- If anything goes wrong, don't scold your girlfriend or boyfriend at the top of your voice.
- Don't say anything to the waiter if the food is not good.
- Don't sit for hours at a restaurant.
- Tip the waiter after clearing your bill.

62

When your Girlfriend/Boyfriend is with You

When you are on your bike or in your car with your girlfriend or boyfriend, then you tend to ride or drive at a high speed. Even your girlfriend or boyfriend feels excited at the speed. But this could be fatal. So don't let this happen. Take care of the following things:

- When you drive, try to keep within the speed limit.
- Don't drive without a driving licence. On your way, the police may ask for it. You will feel humiliated in front of your girlfriend or boyfriend if you don't have a driving licence.
- Wear your seat belt while driving. Also, ask your girlfriend or boyfriend to do so.
- Adjust the mirror before starting, so that the traffic behind is seen clearly.
- Don't overtake other vehicles unexpectedly. Look carefully before overtaking.

- Make use of the mirror at unsafe crossings.
- Don't overtake any vehicle just to impress your girlfriend or boyfriend and always overtake from the right.
- Don't play loud music in the car.
- Don't insist on your girlfriend or boyfriend to learn driving on highways.
- Check petrol, air in tyres, etc. before going out in a vehicle.
- Don't ask your girlfriend or boyfriend to drive and sit at the back yourself.
- Don't try to kiss or hug your girlfriend while driving.
- Concentrate on your driving.
- Follow the traffic rules while driving.
- Don't break signals or queues just for the sake of being a winner.

63

Avoid Making Such Girlfriends/Boyfriends

Many agencies in the country have begun to attract youngsters towards themselves. These agencies, that operate all over the country, are running rackets in the name of providing open friendship to young boys and girls.

If you notice the language used in the advertisement, you will understand the matter and the truth will be out. At one place it is written – 'You are looking for an open-minded person.' At another place it says –'Find a friend of your choice. If you don't find, there is money-back guarantee.' A third advertisement says – 'Enjoy life fully. Dial the number and talk to the friend of your choice.(only for adults).'

You can easily figure out the agencies which are promoting flesh trade in the name of friendship. Don't get in the rut of making such girlfriends, because they will ruin you financially, physically and mentally.

- Beware of such a business of friendship.
- A friendship bought is of no use. It will remain limited to the money.

- Talking to girls or boys on the phone is also a kind of a mental disease called eschatologia. Once you become addicted to it, you cannot get out of it. If you are not careful, you can also be a victim of blackmailing.
- Girls willing to be friends with you in an advertisement are no good. It is a kind of flesh trade.
- There are several sites on the Internet that cater to on-line dating.
- Dating messages have begun to come on the mobile as well. You must avoid such dating.
- Nowadays agencies are giving a new twist to dating by naming it as fast dating. They arrange a place for the meeting of a boy and a girl and they charge them highly for it.
- In the name of dating, these agencies provide girls to boys. They extract a high amount of money from the boys. In return for your money, you can do anything with the girl.
- On Internet, bio-data and photos of many girls are readily available. Those girls are ready to become friends with anybody. The girls look beautiful, but they are cunning. They extract money for their body as well as the time spent.

64

When You Hate Something about Your Girlfriend / Boyfriend

Often a good-looking girlfriend or boyfriend may have several bad habits. In such circumstances, you will be in a difficult situation. So you should have extra patience and tolerance.

- If it hurts you when your girlfriend or boyfriend talks to you bitterly, then find out the cause as to why she or he behaves this way. Do you lack anything? If yes, then try to mend yourself. If her or his nature is like that, then try to talk to her or him gently.
- If your girlfriend or boyfriend criticises others, then tell her or him to change the habit.
- If he or she talks while moving his or her hands, twisting the waist and winking her or his eyes, tell her or him about body language.
- Don't take anything seriously what your girlfriend or boyfriend is saying.
- Don't argue with your girlfriend or boyfriend if you don't like something about her or him.

- Ignoring the trivialities of your girlfriend or boyfriend is a sign of a civilised person.

Be sensible

- Don't doubt if you really love her or him.
- Present your girlfriend or boyfriend a lovely gift on her or his birthday.
- Don't put pressure on your girlfriend or boyfriend to do anything bad.
- Don't praise her beauty only. Praise her personality as well.
- Behave respectfully with her or her brothers, sisters and parents.
- Ignore small mistakes of your girlfriend or boyfriend and take it easy.
- If anybody criticises your girlfriend or boyfriend, give a straightforward reply.
- Support your girlfriend or boyfriend in every situation.
- If your girlfriend or boyfriend praises her or his friend, don't discuss it. Just ignore it.

65

Love-o-Ditation

'Have you ever been in love with someone?'

'Yes, I have.'

'I have been in love too.'

'Have you ever done love-o-ditation?'

What is love-o-ditation ?

A famous German scientist, Shark Nicholic says that love-o-ditation is a kind of meditation. Every lover should do this. It is a meditation and exercise for all lovers. This increases the positive power of love within them. The energy of love multiplies immensely.

- You don't need to spare a long time over this.
- Close your eyes and think about your girlfriend or boyfriend and bring his or her picture in mind.
- Keep your girlfriend's or boyfriend's picture in mind three to four times.
- If the picture of your girlfriend or boyfriend does not get formed, don't panic. It happens so initially. Gradually you will find improvement in this.

- Don't bring negative thoughts into your mind while meditating on your girlfriend or boyfriend.
- Repeat your promise that you will accept her or him in all circumstances.
- You can even talk to your girlfriend or boyfriend while meditating. This will give practice and courage of talking to her or him.
- Love-o-ditation increases the emotions of love in the girl or boy. You get enough love energy.
- You will find yourself quite close to your girlfriend or boyfriend.
- Love-o-ditation makes your face radiant and your heart filled with enthusiasm. The entire body gets stimulated. It gives a different kind of excitement to the entire body.
- Love-o-ditation makes your love profound. You get ample power.

66

Don't Put Your Career at Stake for Your Girlfriend or Boyfriend

After falling in love, many boys put their career at stake. Instead of doing a full-time job, they indulge in full-time love. They spend all their time going to beaches or to restaurants or some other places. The significance of love is in its own place. There's nothing wrong in falling in love, but it is not a good idea to spoil your career for the sake of your girlfriend or boyfriend.

- Remember you can make your life if you have a career. Falling in love is only a part of life.
- It is stupidity to go after your girlfriend or boyfriend, leaving behind your job.
- Don't let your girlfriend or boyfriend spoil your career. This might spoil your life.
- Don't make it your ambition only to please your girlfriend or boyfriend.

- "I will forget the world in your love," is a good thought to have, but don't forget your career.
- Don't waste your time over your girlfriend or boyfriend if you are taking part in any competition or examination.
- If you are well established in your career, your girlfriend or boyfriend will like you. If you destroy your career, she or he will leave you.
- Don't go running to your girlfriend or boyfriend if you miss her or him. Try to control yourself.

Solutions

- Don't spend the entire day with your girlfriend or boyfriend. Decide a particular time and place to meet each other.
- If there is no time, talk on the phone or mobile and adjust yourself.
- You can spend most of the time with your girlfriend or boyfriend on the weekends.
- If you miss your girlfriend or boyfriend, sprinkle water on your face. Go out for a walk.
- To divert your attention, listen to music, read a novel, or a story, or watch a movie.
- Always remember, if you have a job, you will have a girlfriend or boyfriend. If you don't, you will not have one.

- Write, in big letters, on the wall of your study room, sentences like — "I want to be something in life", "I have to concentrate on my career?" etc. By doing so, your eyes will see these sentences again and again and you will not be distracted in life.

67

Why Does This Happen?

The main cause of a break-up of in a love relationship is finding your choice in chaos. In your mind you have a big list of good qualities and bad qualities. It is almost impossible to find all the good qualities together. But you do fall in love even if you are attracted by one or more qualities. If any of the bad qualities of the girlfriend or boyfriend becomes prominent, the attraction is over and your love relationship comes to an end.

Psychologists are of the opinion that the number of lovers who use their brains along with the hearts is dropping at a considerable rate. Psychologists also say that since love is blind, lovers do not even look at the bad qualities. Their falling in love blindly proves that love is blind.

- ♥ Fall in love with a person who gives you the guarantee to support you all your life.
- ♥ Make sure your girlfriend's or boyfriend's behaviour is not mean, because of which you will be humiliated in front of others.

- Staying close to each other will only let you know the likes and dislikes of each other. So dating is the best means. But remember that it should not lead to physical intimacy.
- Stay away from girls or boys who would like to have physical contact before marriage.
- Don't trap anybody, pretending to be in love with him or her or other acquaintances.
- If you don't love somebody, then express it without hesitation.
- Don't make promises of getting the moon and the stars to your girlfriend.

68

Avoid Excess

Excess of everything is bad. Whether it is sports, entertainment, fun, bunking school or figure consciousness, doing anything in excess is considered a mental disease. So avoid extremes even in the matter of love.

- You love your girlfriend or boyfriend very much. Don't tell her or him 100 times that you love her or him. She or he will not like it at all.
- Some boys have the habit of reaching the venue of the meeting much later than the given time. For example, if the scheduled time is 2 o'clock, you go there at 8 o'clock. When your girlfriend reaches there at the scheduled time, you shout at her. And you complain that you have been waiting since morning. "Why have you been so long?"
- Don't repeatedly give your girlfriend or boyfriend expensive gifts. She or he may make a wrong judgement about you.
- Don't disturb your girlfriend or boyfriend and others by

going to her or his house or calling her or him again and again.

- Don't try to set a world record by sending ' I love you' repeatedly on his or her mobile.
- Don't keep your girlfriend or boyfriend till late at night. No parents will like their daughter or son to remain out till late at night.
- Don't tell your girlfriend or boyfriend to take care of her or his figure again. Don't make a lot of fuss about eating by telling not to eat this and not eat that. This will hurt her or him very much.
- Don't insist on going on a long drive again and again.
- Don't keep on nagging your girlfriend or boyfriend again and again. If you do so, she or he may say goodbye to you.
- Be on time wherever you have arranged to meet your girlfriend or boyfriend. If you get delayed or don't make it by any chance, send her or him an SMS and let her or him know about it.

69

When Your Girlfriend is Pregnant

When emotions of love become overpowering, the desire to have sex increases. So love has become a synonym of sex, instead of being considered sacred. If this is so in your case, then it is big problem. So don't let sex come in between love.

When you have a sexual contact, there are chances that your girlfriend will become pregnant. In such circumstances, life becomes stressful. Some boys cannot tolerate such problems and so they ask their girlfriend to go for an abortion, or they go far away from their girlfriend's life. Sometimes, they even accuse her of something bad and try to get rid of her.

When your girlfriend becomes pregnant, you must keep your wits under control. You should not rush into any step that will make you repent later.

- Don't have sexual intercourse when you are alone. It will have dangerous consequences.

- To love is not to deceive. Be faithful in love. You dared to fall in love willingly, so you should have the courage to accept the challenges.
- When your girlfriend becomes pregnant, don't run away, leaving her in trouble. Only cowardly people run away like that. You both are responsible for the trouble. So you must find a solution together.
- Don't find faults with her or traumatise her. Both of you are at fault, so solve the problem together.
- Don't try to get rid of her if your girlfriend insists on getting married instead of aborting the child.
- If you marry her and accept her, your problems will be solved automatically.
- If your family is not willing to accept her, then try to convince them. If they don't accept even after that, then oppose them strongly. Seeing your attitude, they will eventually relent.
- If you are weak financially, try to solve it with the help of your family, relatives and friends.
- Don't go for an abortion by visiting midwives, nurses or quacks. This might prove to be dangerous.
- You loved her and you liked her, so accept and support her under any circumstances. Give the child in her womb the name of its father, that is, your name.

70

Number of Roses

- 1 rose – Love at first sight.
- 2 roses – Mutual understanding.
- 3 roses – I love you.
- 4 roses – I love you unconditionally.
- 10 roses – You are mine and only mine.
- 11 roses – You are the empress of my heart.
- 12 roses – We are together and we will be so forever.
- 13 roses – Our love will always remain.
- 15 roses – Pardon me.
- 20 roses – May our trust remain.
- 21 roses – I will be faithful in love until I die.
- 36 roses – I will be fragrant with the fragrance of your love.
- 40 roses – I love you immensely. I am telling you this.
- 99 roses – I will keep on loving you, only you.

- 100 roses – If you are with me, I don't lack anything.
- 101 roses – You are mine. You cannot be anybody else's besides me.
- 108 roses – Will you marry me?
- 999 roses – Our love will remain as long as there are the sun and the moon.

71

I Love You in Different Languages

English	–	I love you.
Thoruba	–	*Mo nee phe.*
Wallace	–	*Khain de geroo.*
Vietnamese	–	*An yuoo am.*
Urdu	–	*Aapse mohabbat karta hoon.*
Ukranian	–	*Ya tebe kaheyu.*
Turkish	–	*Yenee yevithorum.*
Tamil	–	*Naan attraikathalikrina.*
Tahini	–	*Ue here wau ae oe.*
Taiwanian	–	*Waa gaa ei lee.*
Tegalog	–	*Mehal kita.*
Swiss	–	*German ich leb dee.*
Swedish	–	*Jag alaskar dig.*
Swahili	–	*Ninapenda.*
Spanish	–	*Te kuiro tea mo.*

Slovenian	–	*Jubin te.*
Slovak	–	*Lubin taa.*
Setswana	–	*Ke a go reta.*
Scot Galic	–	*Tha graad etham ort.*
Russian	–	*Yaan tebyalithublasu.*
Roman	–	*Te ubesk.*
Portuguese	–	*Yu tea mo.*
Polish	–	*Kochum sibi.*
Cheyeni	–	*Ne mohotatse.*
Katelin	–	*Tisteemo.*
Bulgarian	–	*Aubicham te.*
Belarus	–	*Yaa taabe keheyoo.*
Bengali	–	*Amee tomake bhalo basee.*
Bambaara	–	*Mabeeke.*
Armenian	–	*Yas kej siruman.*
Finish	–	*Meena rekastan sina aa.*
Hawaii	–	*Ailona wau aae oee.*
Hindi	–	*Main tumhe pyar karta hoon.*
Hyog	–	*Kuv talab koj.*
Hope	–	*Nu umee anangwata.*
Hungarian	–	*Jeretlek.*

Icelandic – *Eg falaska tig.*

Piglatin – *Iae aawle autheyee.*

Persian – *Doset daran.*

Paipiyamento– *Meet a swimabon.*

Paigasinon – *Inaru taakaa.*

Paidekan – *Ruyota ne kita.*

Norwegian – *Jeg alaskar deg.*

Newaho – *Ayor anoshinee.*

Nehotla – *Nee mitsa nekee.*

Mokhkan – *Ana mo ajobaa bik.*

Kohok – *Kambhak.*

Marathi – *Mee tula prem karto.*

Malayalam – *Gyan nine tramikutru.*

Malaysian – *Yayaa chinken mu aku chintaa padmu.*

Lithuanian – *Tavemailisu.*

Lebanese – *Mehilek.*

Latwanian – *Es tevee mailu.*

Latin – *Tea mo.*

Korean – *Serang heyo.*

Konkani – *Tu majel monga cho.*

Kiswahilee – *Neku panda.*

Kapemgan – *Keluguren daka.*

Kannada – *Nanu nitra pritisutene.*

Japani – *Aisiteroo.*

Italian – *Tee amo.*

Irish – *Tramee nava leer.*

Inuite – *Negligewapse.*

Indonesian – *Saya chinta padmu.*

Ingloggo – *Palenga kee ikev.*

Gujrati – *Mu tane prem karu chhu.*

Unani – *Sogapo.*

German – *Ich lege dich.*

Janian – *Mirkwarhar.*

Gelic – *Ta te am je tedar.*

Philipino – *Mehal kita.*

Pharsee – *Dost garam.*

Pherois – *Eg elaski teg.*

Ethopian – *Aphgrephy.*

Estonian – *Maa armaastan sind.*

Esperanto – *Mee amas vin.*

Dutch – *Ak how wain jao.*

Danish	–	*Jeg alasker dig.*
Chek	–	*Miloojee te.*
Croatian	–	*Wolimte.*
Kriol	–	*Mee emi jau.*
Kosiken	–	*Tee tengu karu.*
Chicheva	–	*Deemaku konda.*
Sindhi	–	*Ma tokhe pyar kendo hayaan.*
Arabian	–	*Anaa behibaak anaa bahibaak.*
Cambodian	–	*Soro lahan hanee ehh.*
Baisayaa	–	*Nehee gugmaa ako kanimo.*
Thai	–	*Chaak rak chun* (to a male), *phome rak chun* (to a female).
Telugu	–	*Nenu nitru pramistu trannu.*
Hiligeynon	–	*Penglagga ko ikeva guiina.*
Hebrew	–	*Anee oveh aataah* (to a female), *anee oleh eit osha* (to a male)
Mandarin Chinese	–	*Wo ai nee.*
Cantonese Chinese	–	*Angoaai ne a.*

72

What Celebrities Say about Love

A man learns to live when he falls in love with a woman.

- Hritik Roshan (Filmstar)

It is important to leave 'I' and accept 'we' in order to obtain love.

- Bharat Thakur (Artistic Yoga Expert)

The faster you fall in love, the sooner it will break.

- Aparna Roy Mazumdar (Writer)

If you marry someone you love, then it is wonderful.

- Arbaaz Khan (Filmstar)

It is difficult to contain love in words. In my opinion there is time for everything. It is good to love at the right time.

- Charlie (Model)

Love speaks volumes'. No word is necessary.

- Ravi Sarkar (Fitness Expert)

There is no question of profit and loss in love.

- Awadhesh (Film Director)

If you love someone, it is not necessary that she will also equally love you.

- Bandana Bachpayee (Singer)

If you want true love, then learn to give, not take.

- Jitendra Nagpal (Psychiatrist)

If you love someone, accept her with her good as well as bad qualities.

- Sunidhi Chauhan (Singer)

Love can be a success only when the thoughts of both the partners are the same. And there should be emotional attachment.

- Shivani (Singer)

You fall in love only once in life. In fact there is no ego in love. It demands dedication, not insistence.

- Samanta (Beauty Expert)

If there is restlessness in yor heart about someone, then consider that you are in love.

- Bhavana (Jewellery Designer)

If you are happy, then you fall in love. If you want to remain miserable, then it is certain that nobody's love can make you happy.

- Jatin Kochar (Fashion Designer)

In fact, there is no other thing as good as love.

– Amar Patel (Model)

Love and smile cannot be hidden, cannot be subdued or suppressed and cannot be stopped.

– M. K. Mazumdar (Writer)

73
Love Quotations

- For men love is an expression, for women it is a feeling.

  \- Anonymous

- Men love often, but only a little. Women love less frequently, but in plenty.

  \- Basta

- Love of a man starts with love, but ends in a woman. Love of a woman starts with a man but ends in love.

  \- Anonymous

- Love differs from lust as much as glass differs from gold.

  \- Premchand

- Life is a flower and love is its fragrance.

  \- Victor Hugo

- Love is off the limits of time and place. It is free of control.

  \- Vivekananda

- To love is to mingle one's happiness with the happiness of others.

  \- Leniniz

- Love is courage; love is strength. Love is the infinite way of life.

  - Vivekananda

- Those people, who advertise their love in front of others, love the least of all.

  - Shakespeare

- Love is the sweetest joy of life and bitterest pain of life.

  - Belley

- If you want to be dear, then love and be worthy of love.

  - Franklin

- The entire human society loves a lover.

  - Emerson

- Love is more or less a fruit of marriage.

  - Maulier

- Love is a dangerous mental disease.

  - Plato

- A man becomes blind in love. It is beautiful to find love, but it is more beautiful to give love without being asked.

  - Shakespeare

- The thirst of love cannot be quenched by unlimited amount of water and nor can it be immersed in dangerous flood.

  - Solomon

- To say that you will keep loving a person lifelong is equal to saying that a candle will keep burning as long as you want.

  - Tolstoy

- A heart full of love shows mercy to the person being loved and loves him even when he gets injured.

  - Mahatma Gandhi

- Love is a way to heaven, another name of humanity. To love the entire creature is only true humanity.

  - Gautama Buddha

- We should extend the parameters of love so much that it may include a village, from village to city, from a city to a state, and in this way it can extend all over the world.

  - Mahatma Gandhi

- It is love that runs the world.

  - Anonymous

- Love is painful happiness.

  - Anonymous

- Only he, who has been injured by the arrows of love, understands the power of love.

  - Anonymous

- Like other forms of matter, the origin of love is nature.

  - Allen

- Excessive fuss destroys love.

  - Romain Rolland

- On the foundation of love, there is the union of souls.

  - Shelley

- Come, dwell in my heart and don't pay any rent.

  - Samuel Lover

- To love and to obtain love is the greatest happiness of human life.

  - Sydney Smith

- I am even willing to drink poison in love.

  - Benjamin Franklin

- People go crazy by falling in love, crazy people become sane by obtaining love.

  - Anonymous

- The meaning of love is to mingle one's love with another's happiness.

  - Leniniz

- It is easy to make girlfriend, but it is difficult to keep her.

  - Anonymous

- It is easy to give up life for a lady whom one loves, but it is difficult to live together.

  - Romain Rolland

- If nobody loves you, then take it for granted that you are at fault.

  - Dadriz

- The best way to remain miserable is not to love anybody.

  - George Bernard Shaw

- Don't snap the thread of love. Once it is snapped it cannot be joined. Even if it is joined, there will be a knot.

  - Rahim

- *Dampati sukh aye vishaya ras, puja, nishtha, dhyan,*
  Itne pare bakhaniye shuddh prem Raskhan.

  - Raskhan

- There is no union like that of love.
  Only wood can pierce lotus, a bee cannot.

  - Brinda

- Prem chhipaya na chhipaye, jaa ghat parghat hoye
  Jo pae mukh bole nahi, nain det hain roye.

  - Kabir

Take One More Chance

By Shriya Garg

Price	:	Rs. 125
Pages	:	256
Size	:	5.0×7.75 inches
Binding	:	Paperback
Language	:	English
Subject	:	Fiction/Comedy
ISBN	:	9788183520140

About the book:

Naina Kashyap's to-do List:

1. Change career.
2. Next time the guy at McDonald's acts stupid—be polite. Don't get him arrested again. Stupidity is not a crime. Unfortunately.
3. Change society's notion towards child labour.
4. Dad wants me to get married. What the___?

Also remember to change family.

Some people always take the right decisions and some people take decisions and then make them right.

Naina Kashyap was so sure that she fell in the second category. A sharp-tongued, career-oriented girl of today, she had an opinion about everything—from the local underprivileged children forced to work as labourers to her parents' if-I-am-Jesus-Christ-then-you-are-Paris-Hilton marriage.

So when her father ordered her to find a decent groom for herself, she responded in the only way she knew how—rebellion. From crazy accidents in Delhi's streets to near drowning in kiddie pools, she rained her wrath on every man she came across.

She thought that things could never get worse. Little did she know that the drama had only just begun.

The Promise

By Chital Mehta

Price	:	Rs. 125
Pages	:	240
Size	:	5.0×7.75 inches
Binding	:	Paperback
Language	:	English
Subject	:	Fiction/Romance
ISBN	:	9788183520133

About the book:

Dad says, 'Go to work' (how boring!)

Heart says, 'Have a blast' (yippee)

Dad kicks me out. What do I do now? (Lost!)

Friends are damn busy (Grrrrrr)

I meet Pinky (It's definitely love at first sight, believe me!)

I join CAT class (whoa! I am in love)

My love life rolls on rocking (yeah, she loves me too. Great na?)

Dad is also happy (Son is finally studying. Duh!)

Rani steps in....nice girl, really cute (just a friend!)

She is my best friend but then...she says she loves me...

Oops... I kiss her (I didn't mean to...)

But I love Pinky (Do I?)

And I have made her a promise... (I can't break it)

This is me, Ajay. (Lost and confused madly in love)

Can you really measure friendship and love?

Step into Ajay's world which is filled with frolic, fun, confusions and craziness to discover the truth about friendship and love.

Beyond Love

By Ankit Uttam

Price	:	Rs. 125
Pages	:	224
Size	:	5.0×7.75 inches
Binding	:	Paperback
Language	:	English
Subject	:	Fiction/Romance
ISBN	:	9788183520126

About the book:

If you think that MITs, IIMs and IITs are the be all and end all of the every college.

THEN THINK AGAIN...

Get ready for a roller coaster ride in the coolest college of the country because this year your definitions will take an about-turn and on this highway many romantic hearts will be shattered. Be ready to experience a war between your mind and your heart, for that four letter CUSS word..........LOVE.

Love is not always pure, sacrifice, friendship, cupid, red, saintly or simply a four letter word. Discover the darkest secrets of your heart where love deciphers into lust, betrayal, money, blasphemy, destruction, war, death, evil, myth and a question.

A tale of four and a half love stories and a hell lot of disaster which should not have happened and unfortunately it did happen.

Discover what the hell lies beneath and beyond those four letter word......LOVE?

Just Friends...

By Sumrit Shahi

Price	:	Rs. 125
Pages	:	264
Size	:	5.0×7.75 inches
Binding	:	Paperback
Language	:	English
Subject	:	Fiction/Romance
ISBN	:	9788183520119

National Bestseller

About the book:

He knows everything about her, right from her favourite books to her favourite bra.
She knows everything about him, right from his favourite soccer club to his favourite x rated websites.
He will complete her English homework, even at three in the night.
She will arrange an Armani suit for him, even if it calls for flirting with ugly guys.
He has her picture in his wallet.
She has his number on speed dial.
They talk to each other all the time.
They talk about each other when they don't talk to each other.
They discuss everything from periods to playstation.
They have tasted alcohol and then thrown up...*together.*
They have bunked countless tuitions... *together.*
They can't live without each other.

YET

They don't love each other.
They are **JUST FRIENDS...**

'Just Friends' is funny, honest, sad and straight from the heart.

—The Indian Express

Through his debut novel, Sumrit tries to reflect the mindset of a teenager and the relationship shared between the modern day parents and their children.

—The Hindustan Times

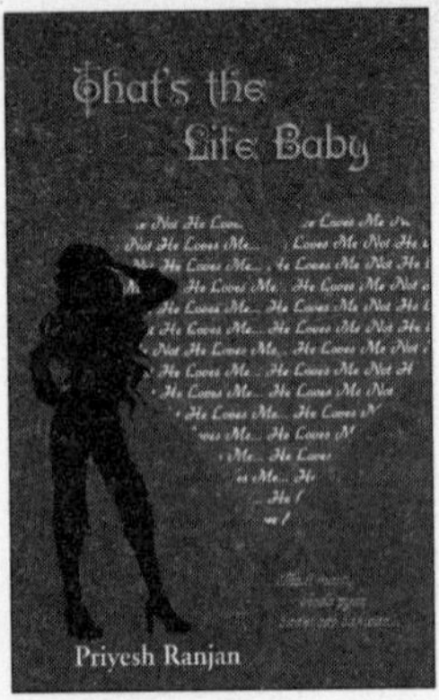

That's the Life Baby

By Priyesh Ranjan

Price	:	Rs. 99
Pages	:	224
Size	:	5.0×7.75 inches
Binding	:	Paperback
Language	:	English
Subject	:	Fiction/Romance
ISBN	:	9788183520003

National Bestseller

About the book:

Sixteen is sweet, Seventeen sweeter and Eighteen is the sweetest!

He thinks so.

What about Love at Eighteen? It happens, everyday! Doesn't it?

True for him!

Have a lot of girls in your life. It feels macho to have options. Girls don't need the advice. They are the wiser sex and have been playing *multi-boying* games for eons.

.....But he has three gorgeous damsels, all envious and shooting high testosterone levels.

How will you thank god if your balcony faces a girls' hostel? .....By being there 24X7? May be!

Exactly what he aims at!

Skirts lead to scandals. Don't they? Ban it or allow scandals.

He loves both, skirts and scandals.

What does he think about 'committed' tag?

You can't keep on eating the same chocolate all the time! Feels like jailed!!!

Meet Abhi. He is one of you with a devil's head! A year at Kota and his life remains no more the same. It all starts with a Bollywood-style love at first sight with Aditi. He sees, he falls, he cajoles and a little luck makes them one! Together they write new rules of dating & romance. Their amorous adventures will make you feel the passion of adolescence. But one day everything changes. How? What? Why? Answers lie in the story.

A stormy honeymoon of emotions......Get ready to laugh and cry!!!

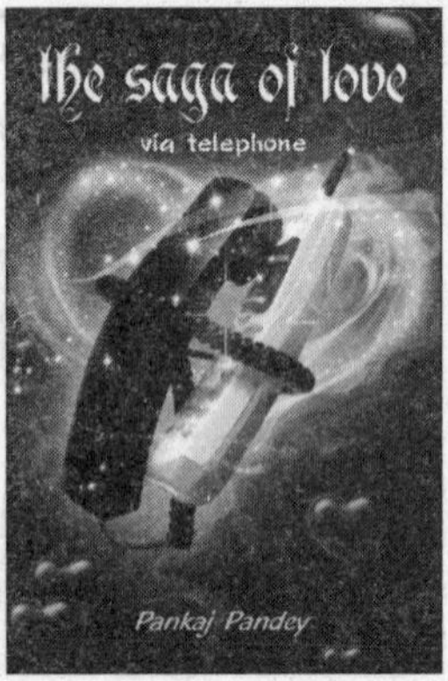

The Saga of Love via Telephone

By Pankaj Pandey

Price	:	Rs. 99
Pages	:	152
Size	:	5.0×7.75 inches
Binding	:	Paperback
Language	:	English
Subject	:	Fiction/Romance
ISBN	:	9788183520669

About the book:

Love means never losing hope...

He is Pankaj, a creative and innovative guy of an engineering college.

She is Shikha, a sensation. Her voice is that of a nightingale.

They fall in love without an eye-contact talk, share everything, foresee future...

Destiny had something in their fate...

This novel takes you to a journey of love, romance, passion, thrill and saturnine events.

About the Author:

Pankaj Pandey, a technocrat turned writer, is an ex-student of Babu Banarsi Das Institute of Technology, Ghaziabad. He is an eloquent speaker and is striving to be successful in the field of leadership, life improvement and consultancy.

Media Reviews:

The Saga of Love is a vibrant and cherished love story. ***Organiser***

A unique love story via the telephonic conversation which is beautifully written by the author. ***Dainik Jagran***

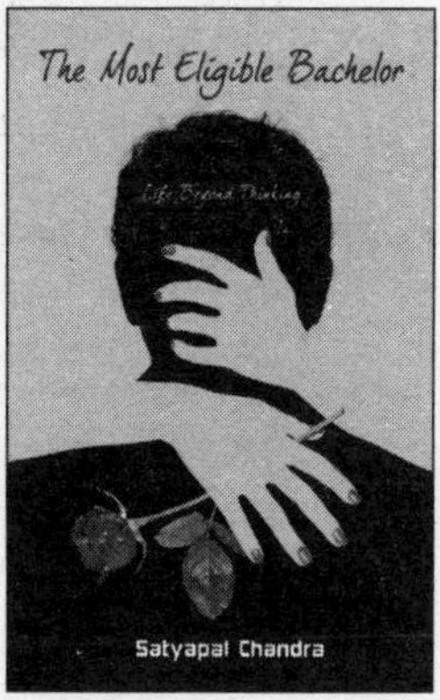

The Most Eligible Bachelor

By Satyapal Chandra

Price	:	Rs. 125
Pages	:	224
Size	:	5.0×7.75 inches
Binding	:	Paperback
Language	:	English
Subject	:	Fiction/Romance
ISBN	:	97881835208051

About the book:

Why do most love stories end with great difficulty? Why do we always claim that he or she cheated in love and caused indelible pain? Is love the name of deep understanding and mutual relationship between two souls or is it just intense desire for physical intimacy? Why does the first love invariably mean sacrifice which is against social and Nature's laws? Why don't people get selfless love in return to their selfless love for one? Why don't people again embark on the journey of love after getting cheated once?

This is an inspiring story of a self-made entrepreneur, who reaches the heights of success after confronting adversity at every step on the journey through recession, unemployment and religious discrimination; a journey through which he loses everything including his love, his best friend and his only mentor and motivator. But do these kill his spirit or his aim in life? Read this story to find answers to this and many other questions.

Legally, Lovingly Yours

By Abhishek Bose

Price	:	Rs. 125
Pages	:	186
Size	:	5.0×7.75 inches
Binding	:	Paperback
Language	:	English
Subject	:	Fiction/Romance
ISBN	:	9788183520195

About the book:

Love-hate-jealousy-admiration-amity-animosity-friendship-enmity—for people in general may be only words, but for eighteen-year old Abhishek Banerjee these words turned out to be life-changing experiences over the next five years.

He harboured dreams of studying in a good college, to make new friends there, to have a girl by his side as his girlfriend, and above all, to carve out a niche for himself and leave his mark. He started realising his dreams when he got selected to study in the Animus Law School, one of the premier private law schools of the country. But, on the very first day he realised that Lady Luck was not on his side.

Could he make new friends as he had yearned for? Did he meet and get the girl he dreamt of? Was he able to make his mark? If no, then why not? If yes, then how?

Blessed with a nature endowed with patience, helpful attitude, desire for friendship, a never-say-die spirit and a never-give-in attitude, Abhishek embarks on a five-year long journey through college and on the way faces all kinds of experiences, both good and bad.